"I have worked alongside Dr. Shelley Uram for many years. She is a brilliant psychiatrist who has the wonderful ability to take complex information and make it practical, relatable, and easily understood. This can apply to the healing of psychological trauma, addictions, poor self-esteem, or whatever the marker is for having disconnected from one's core self. *Essential Living* offers readers a thorough explanation about what the Essential Self is, shows us how we become detached from it, and then expertly guides us to rediscover it. May we all find our authenticity and fulfill our life purpose through Dr. Uram's wise words."

—Claudia Black, PhD
author of *It Will Never Happen to Me,*
Repeat After Me, and *Intimate Treason*

"What is the Essential Self? Dr. Shelley Uram shows us that the connection with our Essential Self is a natural source of vitality, intuition, and our sense of continuity and cohesion. This practical, step-by-step guide provides the everyday tools that we can use to engage and move us along our conscious path in life. As Plato said: 'The life which is unexamined is not worth living.' So this treasure of a book provides us a guide to examine and awaken the one precious life that we have. Read, learn, and participate in this rewarding journey."

—Peter A. Levine, PhD
founder of Somatic Experiencing™ and
author of *Waking the Tiger: Healing Trauma*

"*Essential Living* is a must read for anyone wanting to live a more meaningful life."

—Pia Mellody
author of *Facing Codependence,*
Facing Love Addiction, and
The Intimacy Factor

Essential Living

Essential Living

A Guide to Having Happiness and Peace by Reclaiming Your Essential Self

Shelley Uram, MD

Health Communications, Inc.
Deerfield Beach, Florida

www.hcibooks.com

Library of Congress Cataloging-in-Publication Data
is available through the Library of Congress

© 2017 Shelley Uram, MD

ISBN-13: 978-07573-1960-0 (Paperback)
ISBN-10: 07573-1960-2 (Paperback)
ISBN-13: 978-07573-1961-7 (ePub)
ISBN-10: 07573-1961-0 (ePub)

Publisher: Health Communications, Inc.
     3201 S.W. 15th Street
     Deerfield Beach, FL 33442–8190

Cover design by Jim Pollard
Interior design and formatting by Lawna Patterson Oldfield
Author photo by PhotosbyLeanna.com

This book is dedicated to
the memory of my dear brother Josh,
who taught me to love
no matter what.

"Love doesn't die,
People do.
So, when all that is left of me is love,
Give me away."

—Merrit Malloy, excerpt from "Epitaph"

"This above all:
to thine own self be true . . ."

—Shakespeare

Contents

Part 2: The Way Home

Illustrations

Acknowledgements

Many people helped to make this book a reality. I would like to especially thank . . .

Jim Dredge, who believed in me before I could believe in myself, and who nudged me enough that I finally completed this book. It would not have happened otherwise!

Marcelle Leet, MD, who graciously gave so much of her time and very careful attention to make this a better book.

Mary Hibberd, MD, who helped me through the rough patches.

Joy Collins, RN, who selflessly critiqued each chapter and helped me remain on schedule for completing them.

Terri Gray, MSW, generously helped out with a final round of reading and revising.

Gary Seidler, who went to bat for me and pried open the door to get this book published.

Pia Mellody, for her unwavering support as a mentor and friend throughout the years.

Adyashanti and Carolyn Settle, who helped me find my inner compass and anchor.

Christine Belleris, Senior Editor at HCI Books, who stood by me with kindness and patience as I fumbled and bumbled my way through the process.

I would also like to especially thank Claudia Black, PhD, and Peter Levine, PhD, for their kind words on the cover.

To Paul Barker, MD, Scott Brassart, Mary Ellen Hettinger, Andrea Miller, Frances Statter, Deidre Stewart, and Gary Wolf—many thanks!

Last but certainly not least, I want to thank all of the "teachers" who have been in my life.

Introduction

A Call to Action

As an experienced psychiatrist, I have witnessed an enormous amount of suffering in human beings from all walks of life and all socioeconomic levels. Much of this suffering could be lessened, stopped, or prevented by people having some understanding of how their brain operates, and then taking action with this knowledge.

Suffering does not always manifest from big traumatic events; it can be experienced subtly or not even noticed. Suffering can be blatant, like severe depression, or vague, like the feeling that something is "just not right" in our life and we can't put a finger on it.

Over the course of my career, I have discovered that the overwhelming majority of people who experience ongoing sadness or anxiousness, are often suffering from these symptoms because they have been living their lives out of alignment with who they really are. Psychiatric medications are often prescribed and can be a useful remedy for removing symptoms of emotional unease, at least temporarily. But I often feel as if these symptoms, if approached from a different perspective, can be the "thread" that we follow that often leads us to the underlying problem. Symptoms like sadness or anxiety, when examined or resolved, can lead to a sense of greater freedom and peace.

I do not believe there is anything wrong with taking psychiatric medication, especially in disorders where medication is helpful and offers many people a new lease on life. But when 25 percent of American women in their forties and fifties are taking antidepressant medication, as opposed to other approaches, I suspect there are better long-term solutions for many.

Over the past twenty-five years or so, the field of psychiatry has staked its claim with medication treatment, very often excluding other alternative approaches that can help us get unstuck. Until the early to mid-1980's, most psychiatrists were skilled at using medications and different types of psychotherapy. Due to shifting insurance company rules, and competition with psychologists, social workers, etc., the field of psychiatry ultimately drew a line in the sand and proclaimed their primary "turf" as psychiatric evaluations and medication treatment. Over time, many people came to associate psychiatrists with medications and not other approaches. This evolution saddened me, as my main reason for entering this field was to help others become free of whatever was holding them back from thriving in their lives.

This book is for anyone interested in reconnecting with their

Essential Self. This is not something spacey or "out there"; rather, this is the most *real you* that you could imagine.

The title of this book, *Essential Living*, refers to living from our very essence, which is the truth of who we are. It is *essential* that we do this if we wish to lessen our suffering. The terms "essence" and "Essential Self" are used interchangeably throughout this book. Their meaning is very similar to the concepts of soul, spirit, truth, Authentic Self, Core Self, and others.

The concept of an Essential Self is drawn from Eastern cultures, and is not woven into most Americans' cultural backgrounds. Therefore, it is often perceived as something strange or foreign. Many people will try to fit this concept into something with which they are already familiar, like religion. But depending upon the person's beliefs, the Essential Self may or may not be related to their religious tradition. The Essential Self is simply who you are, in the most real sense.

> *The Essential Self is simply who you are, in the most real sense.*

The "me" that most of us identify as ourselves, is the *conditioned me*. It has little resemblance to who/what we really are. From a very young age, we unconsciously strive for safety and survival through keeping our caregivers' approval, because that is how our ancient survival brain areas have been wired for millions of years. These brain areas have strongly conditioned and molded us since early childhood so we are usually unaware that they are operating. By striving for safety, however, we are subtly directed to be fear-based. For the rest of our lives, when we are survival- and fear-based, we are turning away from our Essential Self.

The term "conditioning" sounds complicated but its explanation is fairly simple. For example, have you ever been driving and suddenly see a police officer on a motorcycle out of the corner of your eye? If you are anything like me, your heart instantly speeds up, your mouth goes dry, and you automatically take your foot off the gas, check your speedometer, and maybe even apply your brakes—even if you weren't speeding or doing anything wrong. Your body may not fully calm down until you realize that the officer is not following you.

This is a fear-based conditioned response. There is no logic to it. Your brain sees a recognized authority figure who can potentially make your life difficult. Your ancient survival brain areas automatically trigger a fight, flight, or freeze response. Period. This is an example of a conditioned response, and could look something like this:

Police officer → fear response

Another simple example of a conditioned response is far less threatening. When we smell certain foods, like hot, fresh popcorn at the movie theater, we might immediately salivate.

A conditioned response is when two or more things get "tied together" in our mind.

Smell tasty food → salivate

A positive conditioned response feels better than a negative one, like the threat of being ticketed, but it is nonetheless still a conditioned response. For example, when we were students and received good grades on our report card or did well at sports, our parents or coaches were likely pleased with us and praised and/or rewarded us in some way. If this happens often enough, we eventually go on to feel good about ourselves when we perform well. A common example of a conditioned negative response that originates from when we are very young could look like this: you get very angry at your sibling and you hit him. Your parents are really upset and scold you. You are frightened and confused the first few times this happens, but after a few more instances with the same results you don't hit your sibling when you are angry because you don't want to feel your parents' wrath and lose their approval.

Many years later, a result could look like this: You become angry at someone but instead of expressing it—even in a healthy way—you stifle yourself out of fear. Ultimately, you may block off angry feelings from even surfacing.

Anger → strike sibling → very upset parents → avoid anger

While you may not realize it, we all have hundreds of thousands of conditioned responses. They typically build into layers. *Ultimately, much of our personality, attitudes, opinions, and behaviors in life have developed from our conditioned responses—both positive and negative.*

A very ancient brain area, called the brainstem, turns many of these conditioned responses into patterns, which can become habits. The patterns and habits we are consciously aware of are often easier to change than those that escape our conscious awareness.

This process of condi-
tioning is one of the ways
our ancient survival brain
areas try to keep us safe,
and how our ancient sur-
vival brain areas ultimately
shape who we become.

This process of conditioning is one of the ways our ancient survival brain areas try to keep us safe, and how our ancient survival brain areas ultimately shape who we become.

But conditional responses are not our true nature or Essential Self. The fight, flight, and freeze responses of the ancient survival brain areas are felt so strongly in our emotions and bodies that they powerfully condition our behavior. They are at the very root of our personalities and behaviors.

From the time we begin to have conscious awareness of ourselves at the age of three months, we automatically do whatever supports our survival, and ensure our ability to thrive in our families. Maintaining a good relationship with our parents or caregivers upon whom we depend to love, feed, and care for us, is part of our survival mechanism. Our brain is strongly wired to do this, as for many years it is only our caregivers who guarantee our survival.

Our elementary school years are an extension of this. We learn how we are supposed to think, act, and feel in order to be successful at school, which is typically an expectation from our parents.

While this might be initially necessary, it can become problematic later in life when it can erode our overall happiness and emotional well-being. From my perspective, the main problem that develops as a result of this kind of conditioned behavior is that we forget who we really *are*. As the conditioned responses exponentially grow in number and complexity over our early years, we lose touch with our Essential Self.

Most adults can't remember who they really are, as their lives have come to revolve around their emotions and conditioned responses, which direct their concepts about themselves and the world around them.

When we were very young, our moment-to-moment and day-to-day experiences were based upon our most authentic *state of being*—the Essential Self. This has little to do with conditioned thoughts, concepts, emotions, or behaviors. Can I describe exactly what our underlying state of being is? No. Describing it would consist of words and concepts. The Essential Self was around long before any thoughts, emotions, or conditioning were present.

For many years, I searched for the truth of who I really am. I initially searched for truth using my intelligence, thinking, and analyzing capabilities. But I've come to see that it doesn't work that way. Our thoughts and words can only take us so far. They cannot ultimately *capture* the state of being that is our true and original nature. Did you ever try to hold a handful of sand? It just runs through your fingers. The same is true about our Essential Self; our thinking and words cannot grasp it. This is very similar to older radios where you have to turn a knob slowly and deliberately to find certain stations. As a result, the Essential Self is at a different frequency than our usual state of conditioning, and we have to "tune in" to it.

If you want to reclaim your most authentic essence, this book is for you.

It covers the following areas:

1. Mankind's most elemental and authentic inborn nature that I will refer to as the Essential Self.

2. Some of evolution's most ancient survival wiring that remains intact and active in the modern human brain and mind.

3. How these ancient survival brain areas short-circuit our connection with our Essential Self, which ultimately leads us to real suffering.

4. What we can do to reclaim and reconnect with our true identity, the Essential Self.

In order to heal from this extremely common problem we need a call to action. Simply reading about this subject is a great start. But for real and enduring healing, the reader must also put some of it into action. Twenty to twenty-five years ago, little was known about the actions we could take to help alleviate this phenomenon. Now there is. Let's waste no more time.

Please note that some of the chapters end with summary Key Points and/or Principles of Essential Living and some do not.

This book also includes some written exercises. Their purpose is to expand the reader's take away experience of this book.

In general, reconnecting with the Essential Self can be gradual, sudden, or anywhere in between. For many people, letting this process evolve as it needs to, without pushing it, can be a wise path.

This book is an overview of my perceptions of how we might go about reconnecting with our Essential Self. It's not intended to be blindly utilized as a personal guide or prescription. Instead, it's important to reflect on the information provided and find what is true for you. Consulting with a professional is often valuable and, for some, a must.

Finally, I would like to share two things with you. The first is a true story from a time-lapse video that I saw several years ago, and the second is from a well-known children's bedtime story.

The video was of a butterfly trying to emerge from a normal cocoon with the caterpillar turned butterfly still inside. It was just beginning to push and struggle against the cocoon wall to get out. A scientist took a pair of fine scissors and gently cut a small slit in the cocoon wall so the butterfly wouldn't have to struggle so much to get out. With relative ease, the butterfly crawled out of the cocoon. Unfortunately, its wings were bulging with excess fluid. The butterfly staggered all over and couldn't become airborne. It died soon after.

My point? The butterfly needed to struggle to escape the cocoon. That struggle is nature's mechanism designed to squeeze the excess fluid out of its wings and enable flight.

And so it is with us. We need to struggle to squeeze the excess (our false self) away from our true essence (our Essential Self). Without this struggle, we can never fully become who we truly are. In this way, the struggle is a hidden blessing.

One of the ideals most of us grew up with is that we should strive for a comfortable, easy life. In fact, this belief is a part of our culture. It is also part of our biological wiring to avoid pain and seek pleasure. However, this flies in the face of a deeper truth—that struggle is good. It helps us learn. It separates the wheat from the chaff. It helps us to find and appreciate our Essential Self.

Think back to some of the most difficult experiences you've had in life. Haven't they also been some of your greatest teachers?

I also want to mention an old children's story, "The Princess and the Pea." A prince's mother, the queen, wanted to test if a young woman was truly a princess and if she was fit to marry her son. So the queen placed a little pea on the floor and stacked twenty mattresses, followed by twenty down beds on top of the pea, and bid the potential princess a good night. In the morning, the queen asked the girl how she slept. The girl told her she slept very poorly, as something somewhere in the bed had kept her awake all night. She just couldn't sleep. Her extreme sensitivity proved to the queen, beyond a doubt, that she was truly a princess.

A part of this story is analogous to each of us; we are never fully comfortable until we discover and reclaim our true self. Until then, we always have some degree of discomfort and dissatisfaction with our lives—even if we can't quite put our finger on it—a certain sense of deep contentment is missing.

Finally, many terminally ill patients I have met soon before they died described experiencing clarity about their true nature. Many of them expressed regret that they had not had this clarity earlier in their lives, and had been too busy and focused on other matters to make this a priority.

So I ask you now, why wait?

Part 1:

Losing Our Way

Chapter 1

Finding What You Want Most

(It's Probably Not What You First Think)

Angela was a fifty-eight-year-old woman who came to see me four years after her husband, Ted, had suddenly died. They had been a very happy couple. Their children were grown and starting their own adult lives, and Angela and Ted were very content in each other's company. They both enjoyed good health and were avid travelers and hikers. Suddenly, in the middle of a trip to Boston, Ted died of a heart attack while asleep.

Ted had been the center of Angela's life, and his sudden death left her devastated. Four years later, she was still grieving and suffering from the loss. She cried frequently and kept all of his belongings close by.

After reconnecting with her Essential Self through different practices and therapy, her Essential Self assumed its rightful role as her true center. Angela's active grieving for Ted finally resolved. She was able to feel joy when recalling times with him that used to leave her feeling nothing but pain. She began giving away some of his old belongings and felt happy that others benefitted from those items. She particularly enjoyed seeing her nephew's face light up when she gave him Ted's golf clubs.

The quiet, deep strength and resilience of Angela's Essential Self was now present. She was able to successfully refocus her life and find real meaning in activities that were not related to Ted. She no longer felt that her "center" was missing.

The basic premise of this book is that, in our culture, most of the unhappiness and suffering that people go through is based on having lost their connection with their innermost self—the Essential Self. There is no substitute for the quiet, deep strength and resilience that is inherent to it. When we are disconnected from our innermost core, we constantly seek connection and fulfillment from other things and people. We never find this alternative fulfillment, however, because there is no substitute for our Essential Self.

Most of the unhappiness and suffering that people go through is based on having lost their connection with their innermost self— the Essential Self.

As a result of our ancient survival brain areas having not yet evolved adequately to accommodate life for modern humans, our attention begins to get pulled away from our Essential Self. This begins when we are young children. We progressively become more and more attached to learning how to survive and thrive in the family and world around us, e.g., schools, jobs, friends, etc. We forget our Essential Self. Yet, this is our only true "rock" or anchor, which keeps us deeply rooted and gives us a consistent sense of love, peace, connectedness, and the sense that "all is well" even when it is not. The Essential Self not only grounds us and keeps us steady but also provides a compass that points us in the right direction to find resilience in weathering the stresses and strains of life.

By the time we are young adults, we believe our emotional well-being and security are dependent upon our lives working well in certain ways. These could include being healthy, having successful relationships, achieving financial success, etc. Very few people regard conscious connectedness with their Essential Self as part of their well-being.

Inevitably things *do* go wrong; that is just a part of the human condition. We age or get injured; a loved one becomes ill or dies; we lose jobs or money; or relationships become problematic. Similarly, as we mature, we may not meet our ideals of who we think we should be. In these situations, our ancient survival brain wiring believes we are in serious trouble and sets off deep, uncomfortable emotional reactivity in the form of flight, fight, or freeze reactions. We suffer. We will go into much more detail about each of these points as we move through the book.

For now, let's begin at the beginning, by figuring out where you are *right now* as far as identifying what is most important to you. This will be used to tap us into that early childhood thinking that our mind began creating to help us survive. This was when our attention began shifting away from the Essential Self.

In a few pages, we'll begin the first exercise. In order for you to most accurately capture where your thinking is right now, I don't want you to be influenced or biased by what you think your answer *should* be.

So, just for now, don't read anything past the exercise below. Your thinking will change as you read on. If you lock in your initial answer now, you will likely get much more out of the next exercise that appears later in this chapter.

Your answer is your starting point from which we begin this process of self-discovery.

A few caveats: try your best to make sure your answer is not coming from any "shoulds." This could be one of your own shoulds, or those from the family you grew up with, or those from friends, or religious traditions, etc.

When answering the question below, dig down deep and ask yourself what you want *more than anything*. Make sure your answer is *very real* for you. You can tell if it's real for you if it has "juice" powering it and if you *really* want it. The "shoulds" don't usually have much juice attached, but they may sound nice or like what you should want.

One analogy might be when someone declares that they prefer broccoli when what they really want most is chocolate ice cream. They may sort of like broccoli, but it's more of a "should"—something they know is healthy and nutritious. But chocolate ice cream may be where the real juice is for you. Similarly, stay away from "ideal" answers, as these are really just a variation of the shoulds! Also, try your best to avoid giving what you think would be the "right" answer. *The only correct answer is that which is most true for you.* Feel free to read on after you get your answer narrowed down to one sentence. Why is it so important to get clear on exactly what it is that you most want? Because if you want to move in the direction of finding your Essential Self, you really have to know the truth of where you are right now. For example, if you want to get to Point B, you have to know where you are coming from—Point A—in order to move in the correct direction. We begin at the beginning, which is where you *truly* are right now.

When I ask people my standard Essential Self question, "What do you want more than anything in your life?" here are some typical *initial* answers:

More money
Success
To be loved
To be respected
Happy children
Healthy children
Nice house and/or car
Loving relationships
Happy spouse
Certain careers

Marriage

Divorce

To lose weight

To gain weight

Fame

To be valued by others

You get the idea. In contrast, the people who start out with answers like peace, love, joy, etc., usually aren't connecting with the juice of their experience. These are very general concepts. Therefore, when they proceed to the next exercise later in this chapter, which is the *big* one, they quickly get short-circuited because they were mistaken in their Point A; they hadn't followed the juice.

When we move to the next exercise at the end of this chapter, you will follow your juice from your answer below, all the way to its end. By that point, your answers usually come close to touching on the Essential Self.

Stop reading here and answer the following question. Again, don't read past this exercise until you have finished filling it in to your satisfaction.

What do you want more than anything in your life?

Fill in your answer below:

_____

_____

_____

Challenge yourself to narrow it down to one simple sentence, and write that here:

_____

_____

_____

All done? Read on . . .

What Is the Essential Self?

I don't mean anything mystical or pie-in-the-sky when I talk about the Essential Self. I'm referring to the "you" that is the absolute most real and authentic. This real you is not based on who/what you think you *should* be. It's not based on your knowledge, thoughts, feelings, experiences, beliefs, or expectations. It's just who you are, minus all of the above. *Period.* It's really quite simple, yet initially challenging to find.

Have you ever noticed how peaceful it is when you stop—even for just a moment—all pretense, and any effort at all toward trying to make things happen a certain way? Most of the time, we don't let go of all of this trying to control things or get others' approval until we are at a point of giving up or total surrender. And then there is this wonderful peace, even if it is just momentary, when we are just ourselves. For most folks, our mind then quickly re-enters the scene and is off and running again, trying to make something better, or different; trying once again to take the reins and regain control.

As a general rule of thumb, the closer people get to reconnecting with their Essential Self, the more they notice the following in their lives:

Resilient inner strength

Greater wisdom

Greater calm

An increased sense of well-being

An inner stillness

A sense of feeling freer

A greater sense of inner peace

More empowered

More spontaneous

A greater sense of connectedness with others

Increased happiness

More loving of self and others

Perceiving everything through a lens of truth

. . . and much more.

These are the inherent qualities we all have. It sounds like a magic elixir of some kind, but when you reconnect with your Essential Self these things will not only appear in your life more frequently, they will also remain there longer.

Why Do We Disconnect from Our Essential Self?

Beginning at a very young age, our human brain develops and operates in ways that divert our attention away—often very far away—from our Essential Self. Regardless, this essence remains present and available at all times. Most of us have long ago forgotten who we are at our very core.

Unfortunately, the further we turn away from our Essential Self, the more symptomatic we become. This can show up in myriad ways. Just think, if a dog tried to act like a cat all the time, it would just be a matter of time before it became physically and emotionally ill. A dog is not a cat. It suffers if it tries to be a cat. We are not our conditioned mind or personality that develops from it; our true nature is that of our Essential Self. It is only a matter of time before we suffer from acting like something we are not.

We are not our conditioned mind or personality that develops from it; our true nature is that of our Essential Self. It is only a matter of time before we suffer from acting like something we are not.

The "software" that organizes parts of our ancient survival brain has not kept pace with how human beings have evolved and how we live today; it is *very* outdated. It cannot discern between life-threatening experiences that one might have encountered eons ago—like the roar of a lion before he gives chase—from the ho-hum daily stresses and strains of modern life. For example, raised voice of an unhappy spouse or boss that signals the start of an argument. Ultimately, this outdated software creates enormous emotional and psychological baggage for most of us. We end up existing within a very limited scope, almost a straightjacket, of how we experience life and ourselves. Since mankind's current experience is at extreme variance with our most basic inborn nature, the average person suffers. This suffering almost always leads to some type of self-medicating, such as the internet or television, alcohol and other substances, shopping, chronic busyness, food, etc., which often lead to addiction. Addiction creates another obstacle to reconnecting with our Essential Self, and another source of suffering.

What Is the "False Self"?

This is the self with whom we identify from early childhood, as our attention begins turning away from our Essential Self. This leads to progressively developing our identity and personality by trying to gain the love and approval of others as a means to feel safe and secure. At first, it is our primary caregivers, with whom we try to win love and approval by behaving certain ways. Then we try to fit in with our peers when we are school-age.

By the age of three-and-a-half, areas of our brain develop that very strongly influence our attention's shift away from our Essential Self and toward the false self. Through conditioning and forming habits, the false self increasingly becomes our

Through conditioning and forming habits, the false self increasingly becomes our identity. Ultimately, our adult personality, behavior patterns, and coping mechanisms are heavily based on this false self.

identity. Ultimately, our adult personality, behavior patterns, and coping mechanisms are heavily based on this false self. This is very different than our Essential Self, which we have long forgotten about.

Why Is Reconnecting with
Our Essential Self So Important?

The Essential Self is what most of us want out of life—maybe not initially in our conscious awareness, but deep down, at our core. When you begin to remove some of the blockades created by our out-of-date ancient survival brain, you will likely find your Essential Self calmly awaiting your return. It is my hope that this book may expand your understanding of the big picture.

Now, we are moving on to the main exercise. You will be "plugging in" your earlier answer into this section. This exercise is taking your original "Point A" answer, the one that has the "juice," and distilling it down to a deeper truth.

Before you work on yours, here are four examples:

Consider my conversation with Zach, a forty-two-year-old attorney:

> **Me:** What do you want more than anything in your life?
>
> **Zach:** I want to be a really successful attorney.
>
> **Me:** If you are a really successful attorney, what will that give you?
>
> **Zach:** More respect from the other attorneys.

> **Me:** If you get more respect from the other attorneys, what
> would that give you?
>
> **Zach:** A good feeling about myself, like I've arrived.
>
> **Me:** And if you've arrived, what would that give you?
>
> **Zach** (after a pause): Peace. I would have a sense of peace.

Now consider my conversation with Luci, a mom and real estate broker:

> **Me:** What do you want more than anything in your life?
>
> **Luci:** For my children to be healthy and happy.
>
> **Me:** If your children are healthy and happy, what would that
> bring you?
>
> **Luci:** I wouldn't worry so much.
>
> **Me:** If you don't worry so much, what would that bring you?
>
> **Luci** (after a pause): Peace.

Here's my conversation with Mark, an entrepreneur:

> **Me:** What do you want more than anything in your life?
>
> **Mark:** I want to be worth $30 million by the time I'm fifty.
>
> **Me:** If you are worth $30 million by the time you are fifty,
> what would that do for you?
>
> **Mark:** I'd know I'm really successful, that I'm one of the big
> players.
>
> **Me:** If you are one of the big players, what would that bring you?
>
> **Mark:** Like, . . . I'm free.

And finally, my conversation with Adele, a sixty-year-old grandmother and nurse:

Me: What do you want more than anything in your life?

Adele: I want to work less.

Me: If you could work less, what would that give you?

Adele: I could spend more time with my grandkids.

Me: If you spend more time with your grandkids, what would that bring you?

Adele: I feel love and happiness when I'm with them. Joy.

When I asked my first question, "What do you want more than anything in your life?" to four different people, I got four different yet fairly typical responses. Zach told me he wanted to be a really successful attorney; Luci told me she wanted her children to be healthy and happy; Mark said he wanted to be worth a lot of money by the time he turned fifty years old; and Adele said she wanted to work less. All of these are admirable external goals—success, family, wealth, and less work stress—but none of these initial answers struck at the true essence of what they really want most in their lives.

However, with guided questioning, each of these wonderfully unique people was able to distill his or her initial response to its purest and most essential form. Zach's desire for career success boiled down to a desire for *peace*. Luci's desire for healthy and happy kids boiled down to a desire for *peace*. Mark's desire for financial success boiled down to a desire for a *sense of freedom*. Adele's desire to work less boiled down to *love, happiness, and joy*.

I have asked thousands of people this question. However varied their initial answers may be, almost 100 percent of their answers boil down to the inherent qualities of the Essential Self. The five most common final answers are peace, happiness (joy), a sense of freedom, a sense of connectedness, and love.

Let's take a closer look at each of these . . .

Peace

A sense of peace can exist on a continuum. For example, the relative peace we feel after a difficult or uncomfortable situation ends is usually potent but short lasting. That is not the type of peace I'm talking about in conjunction with the Essential Self. With the Essential Self, peace is at the other end of the continuum. This kind of peace runs deeply enough that even negative situations and other life setbacks do not disturb it. This peace is resilient, enduring, and much deeper than the surface ups and downs of life. It's like the stillness deep in the ocean; the waves and agitation at the surface don't even touch it!

Over the years, almost every great spiritual leader has spoken in one form or another about this type of peace. Some have attributed the Buddha as saying, "Peace comes from within. Do not seek it without." Others have said, "We can never have peace in the outer world until we find peace within ourselves." These great people are speaking about peace as it relates to the Essential Self, asking us to dig deep into our core to find the essence of who we really are. Remember, we do not generate peace, we uncover it.

We do not generate peace, we uncover it.

A Deep Sense of Happiness or Joy

Like peace, true happiness is an "inside job." It is not dependent on things outside of us. Even if things aren't going well, basic happiness is still present. This kind of happiness tends to emerge from a deep "well" of happiness and joy that are our most basic nature, rather than anything that is happening or not happening in our lives. This type of happiness is from the inside out and is resilient.

A Sense of Freedom

When I talk about a sense of freedom, this is not necessarily literal freedom, for example, leaving a job or a relationship that feels like bondage. Deeper in most people's psyche is the desire for an *inner sense* of freedom. Someone can be strapped with a job they are not thrilled with, and have real stressors at home, yet walk around with a wonderful sense of inner freedom. Again, this sense of freedom springs from the basic nature of our Essential Self rather than anything outside of us.

Connectedness or Unity

As far as the Essential Self is concerned, feeling connected is not a transient thing. That type of connection is dependent on things and people looking and behaving the way we want them to look and behave. This type of superficial connection is common in our culture. When things don't go our way, we "fall out of like (or love)" with a particular situation or person.

With the Essential Self, however, I'm referring to a sense of being connected that transcends the superficial aspects of a person or situation. This type of connection is an ongoing feeling of oneness with the world and everything in it, flaws and all. When we feel connected in this way, the flaws don't bother us very much. As such, this type of connection is not influenced by surface elements; rather, it arises from the Essential Self.

Love (and Truth)

What I'm referring to here is more of a sense of love that transcends the superficial aspects of the person or situation. It is usually based upon a sense of oneness and the sense that even though we are all flawed, that is just fine. I call this "transcendent love."

Although not listed as one of the five qualities, truth is actually the principle that underlies the others. For example, to answer the questions in the exercises, we look within to find what is true for us.

When you dig down for answers you will turn the spotlight of your attention within to deeper and deeper levels of yourself. This questioning process helps us get closer and closer to our truth. Remember, truth is the nature of the Essential Self.

Love and truth are the two most basic and inherent features of the Essential Self. The other qualities, i.e., sense of happiness, freedom, peace, and a sense of unity, are natural byproducts of love and truth.

Now it's your turn to dig down as I did with Zach, Luci, Mark, and Adele. When you dig down for answers you will turn the spotlight of your attention within to deeper and deeper levels of yourself. This questioning process helps us get closer and closer to our truth. Remember, truth is the nature of the Essential Self.

What do you really want more than anything in your life? Caveat: similar to the original warning from your initial answer earlier in this chapter, you might be tempted to skip over some of your steps by jumping straight to qualities of the Essential Self. For example, you might want to immediately answer "peace" or "happiness." And that may in fact turn out to be your ultimate answer. But jumping straight to the endgame won't actually help you in this exercise. Instead, work the process from start to finish by following your juice each step of the way. Focus on what feels real and meaningful for you in this very moment.

Let's begin.

What do you want more than anything in your life? (Transfer your answer from the earlier exercise.) Make sure you narrow your answer down to one sentence, if you haven't yet done so.

_____

_____

_____

_____

Sit quietly and calmly to answer these questions . . . If you had this (the answer you just gave), what would it give you?

_____

_____

If you had this (the answer you just gave), what would it give you?

_____

_____

If you had this (the answer you just gave), what would it give you?

_____

_____

If you had this (the answer you just gave), what would it give you?

_____

_____

In case you haven't figured it out, you need to repeat this line of questioning until you can carry it no further. Eventually, try to end up with a one-word answer. Write that answer below.

_____

Most likely the answer you just gave contains one or two of some of the qualities of the Essential Self. If not, don't worry. You will likely gain greater and greater clarity as you read on.

Another important point: the initial desires that Zach, Luci, Adele, Mark, and you identified at the beginning are not any worse or better than the deeper desire that was ultimately revealed to you from the boiling down process. However, if we seek the more superficial goals to the exclusion of our deeper soul-level desire to reconnect with our Essential Self, then we may be climbing the ladder of our life with it resting on the wrong wall. Check where you've placed your ladder before you spend more time, attention, and energy climbing it.

Again, it's fine to seek any goals you want, whether to become a well-respected attorney, successful entrepreneur, a great parent, a happy grandparent, etc. Go after whatever you want in life, but also keep your attention on your Essential Self, as there is no substitute for this!

When most of our time, effort, and attention go into seeking something in our external world—to the exclusion of our Essential Self—many people tend to reach the end of their lives with a sense of regret that they hadn't done the inner work of reconnecting with their Essential Self earlier.

As I briefly mentioned in the Introduction, the overwhelming majority of people I've had the honor of speaking with soon before they passed on stated the same thing. They each described that since death was to come soon, they had become aware that their priorities had been incorrect. Self-inquiry about what was most important to them and their life, and then *aligning their life with this priority* in the short time they had remaining, was what really counted. Almost all of them expressed regret that they hadn't had these realizations earlier in their lives.

The common pattern showed that they had lived their lives primarily out of trying to gain others' approval, keep their own approval, keep their families happy, etc. Once they found out their life was ending, they described a sudden clarity for what is really important to them.

*We are here to wake up
out of the outdated and
over-reactive survival
brain dream. Please
don't wait until the end
of your life.*

We are here to wake up out of the out-dated and over-reactive survival brain dream. Please don't wait until the end of your life.

Key Points

1. What almost all of us really want most is to reconnect with our Essential Self. This usually starts out as a deep, unconscious desire.

2. Most of us have long forgotten our Essential Self by the time we are adults.

3. It usually takes some digging to find it.

4. Many of us have put the ladders that we are climbing in our lives against the wrong wall.

5. Many of us don't realize what we have done until we are at the end of our lives.

6. Let us seize the opportunity now to reconnect with our Essential Self.

Principles of Essential Living

- *Most people are not aware of what they most deeply want.*

- *It is essential that we clarify to ourselves what we want most. This determines our life's direction; our lives unfold in this direction.*

- *Ultimately, we all want the same thing; to reconnect with our Essential Self (our true and inherent nature).*

- *Our Essential Self is who we are no matter what; we don't earn it, learn it, buy it, grow into it, or achieve it. We are born with it, and we will die with it, unchanged.*

- *Knowing who we really are is probably the most important task of our lives. It is the Essential Self that can lead us to the best paths and choices we can make during our lifetime. When our identity becomes aligned with the wisdom and knowingness of the Essential Self, it becomes a most valuable life compass.*

- *As we reconnect with our Essential Self, our inherent qualities of love, happiness, a sense of freedom, peace, and a sense of unity emerge, as well as other qualities.*

Chapter 2

The Big Picture

In Chapter One, we learned the difference between the Essential Self and the false self. We have considered what the Essential Self is, versus the false self that we have come to think we are. The very powerful ancient survival brain areas are what ultimately led to the creation/development of the false self and our turning away from the Essential Self.

Now that you have completed the exercises in the last chapter, you are on track to having a much better understanding of what you really want most in life.

As I've discovered in my work, what nearly everyone wants most is to reconnect or reclaim their Essential Self. Most people are not conscious of this, and their deep desire often becomes self-evident as they near death, or are in crisis situations.

To help us understand the bigger picture and avoid having this happen, it is helpful to know how your brain is wired. Let us take a step back and look at the big picture . . .

In the field of psychology, there is a very well-known diagram called "Maslow's Hierarchy of Needs." [1]

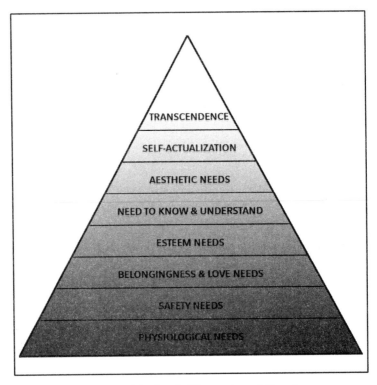

Figure 1: Maslow's Hierarchy of Needs.

In 1943, psychologist Abraham Maslow published a paper entitled "A Theory of Human Motivation." [2] He proposed that over the course of our lifetime we evolve through different levels of needs. *We are usually not aware that these needs motivate what we most strongly seek.*

For example, when we are infants, our deepest need is physiologic stability—maintaining good body temperature, food intake, being held, eye-gazing, staying dry, etc. These basic physiological needs drive our motivation, but we are not aware that these needs are motivating us.

When we become a little older, and our bodies and brains have matured a bit more, and our caregivers are at least adequate, safety becomes our greatest need. For example, we want more than anything to remain connected with our parents. We also we need to be stopped from running into the street, putting our fingers in wall plugs, jumping on the dog, etc. Again, we are not aware these needs are motivating us.

When our brain matures more, and our caregivers continue to be at least adequate, we move up the hierarchy to "Belongingness" needs, "Love" needs, "Esteem" needs, etc.

However, there may be many times in our lives where we temporarily regress and drop back down the hierarchy. A common example can be seen when children undergo stresses that overwhelm them, such as the birth of a younger sibling who takes the attention of their caregiver. The child might temporarily drop back down to a lower level on the hierarchy. Or when people undergo overwhelming stresses, like natural disasters, being a crime victim, etc., they commonly regress back to an earlier level, but it is usually temporary.

For the purposes of this book, the most important levels are the top two: "Self-Actualization," and "Transcendence."

Please note that I am using Maslow's diagram for a starting point and very basic framework, but how I apply it to the Essential Self is independent of Maslow's work.

Those who reach "Self-Actualization" have mastered that which they have consciously sought the most. In the earlier case examples, Zach wanted to actualize being a top-notch attorney, and Luci wanted to actualize being a mother who could raise happy, healthy children.

Whatever you identified in the first exercise as what you want most for your life would be what represents self-actualization for you.

The Essential Self leads us to Transcendence, and is actually a part of Transcendence.

If we go one step further to your ultimate answer at the end of the boiling-down process, we are now within the realm of the Essential Self. The Essential Self leads us to Transcendence, and is actually a part of Transcendence.

Transcendence occurs when we go beyond personal goals and desires, and into something greater than ourselves as we know it.

So, what part of our brain *supports* our having these upper two levels of Maslow's hierarchy? Let's take a very brief look at the three main levels of the human brain, and then you can decide which one best supports finding the Essential Self.

Before we look at the brain, please note that I will often sacrifice accuracy for simplicity wherever I explain brain anatomy and "circuits" in this book. The reality is that this subject matter is extraordinarily complex and can very easily bog you down. Therefore, I am simplifying most of it so that you can walk away with a real understanding of this material.

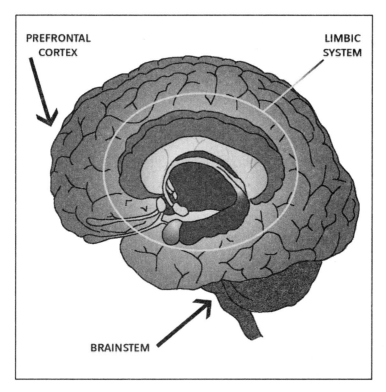

PREFRONTAL
CORTEX

LIMBIC
SYSTEM

BRAINSTEM

Figure 2: The Three Main Levels of the Human Brain.

Brainstem: This is the most ancient part of our brain. On the lower end, it connects with the spinal cord, and on the upper end, it connects with the limbic and other brain areas. It is thought to have originated as far back as 300 million years ago in jawless fish and other primitive animals. Even though it has since evolved into a much more complex brain area, it still maintains similar basic purposes. The brainstem is the master regulator of the brain and the entire body. It keeps everything in balance and running smoothly, such as our chemical balance, breathing, sleep, and certain reflexes, just to name a few. Its operations are 100 percent unconscious. It also has the capacity to shut down our whole system and put us into "freeze" mode, or immobilization, when we are faced with a life-threatening situation. This could look like fainting, "deer in the headlights," etc. In other mammals, this is when the animal appears dead, as often a predator is not interested in eating an animal that is already deceased. When in this severe shut-down state, we feel little to no pain and are at greater ease with possibly dying. Many people in car accidents described the comfort they felt immediately after impact. It was only after this severe shut down lifted that they felt present again, and could feel pain, fear, etc. On the less severe end of the spectrum, which is far more common, freeze can look like spacing out, feeling emotionally constricted, depressed, etc.

Does this sound like it is the primary area of the brain that supports our ascent up to Self-Actualization and Transcendence? Not likely.

Limbic brain: This part of our brain mainly evolved as water-based animals were adapting into land-dwellers. To optimize their chances of surviving, they needed a far more versatile range of survival mechanisms beyond the freeze mode. The fight and flight responses became more evolved. Therefore, the limbic areas of our brain support these survival responses. In addition, the drives for hunger, reproduction, shelter, companionship, safety, etc. originate from the limbic brain areas.

Does this sound like the main brain area that supports Self-Actualization or Transcendence? I think not.

Prefrontal cortex: That leaves us with the newest brain area in our evolution—the prefrontal cortex and several related areas. These areas have numerous functions. The following is a partial list:

- *Paying attention, observing, analyzing, organizing, logic, basic understanding, sense of time, planning, anticipating.*

- *Representational memory, the "story" of our lives, personality.*

- *Impulse control, inhibiting actions that are not appropriate, some emotional regulation, self-control.*

- *The context of an experience, some of our social skills, ability to mediate, negotiate, and weigh possible judgments.*

- *Empathy, ethics, morality, wisdom, personal will, intentions.*

- *Higher Consciousness: access to a sense of joy, peace, love, acceptance (not resignation), sense of oneness, serenity, equanimity, even-mindedness, sense of "all is well" (even if it is not), altruism (but not when it is from a "should"), ability to surrender to something greater than ourselves, gratitude, etc.*

Figure 3: Some Functions of the Prefrontal Cortex in Humans.

Could this be the brain level that best supports our maturing into Self-Actualization and Transcendence?

Ding ding ding! Yes! We have a winner!

While all parts of our brain are vital to our overall health and well-being, in terms of reclaiming our Essential Self, the prefrontal cortex is the brain area we most need. Whether it is actualizing what is primarily important to us and/or transcending beyond that, it is the prefrontal cortex and related areas that grease the way for us! The second half of this book will go into detail about supporting the prefrontal cortex's ability to function well, and how to get it back online when it is not functioning as it should.

The general idea is that we humans are equipped with extraordinarily powerful survival brain circuits. This is a double-edged sword because while these circuits do a great job in protecting us, they also can interfere terribly with other circuits. Some of these other circuits are the ones that give us access to our deep life purpose and Essential Self.

Important: When our lower two brain areas, the brainstem and/or limbic brain areas, become activated into fight, flight, or freeze, either in the short-term or chronically, much of our prefrontal cortex functioning does not operate well. We refer to this as the prefrontal cortex going "offline." Therefore, we can easily become derailed from our life's purposes.

This mechanism of shutting down the prefrontal cortex is helpful to other species, which need to take immediate auto-pilot action when faced with a threat. Stopping to think in such a situation could result in serious injury or death to the animal. In the case of humans, however, this prefrontal cortex area also supports some of our most highly developed functions. Therefore, we also lose those functions when we perceive a threat. I consider this an evolutionary brain "glitch" that has created most of our greatest problems. The rest of this book explains it further, and what we can do about it.

Key Points

1. Maslow's Hierarchy of Needs captures the deep, underlying needs that motivate us through the different stages of our lives. If all goes well, we gradually proceed through these and ultimately actualize, or bring to fruition, that which is very important to us. Many people go beyond that, where they transcend the limited self, and come to recognize the Essential Self.

2. To reconnect with our Essential Self, we worked our way through the exercises in the previous chapter that helped us initially identify what we think we want most, and then boiled that answer down to what we want most at a deeper level. These two answers are aligned with the uppermost two levels of Maslow's hierarchy: Self-Actualization and Transcendence. The greater we align the living of our lives with these two levels of needs, there is potentially enormous power and energy.

3. In order for us to consistently align our lives with what is most important to us, our prefrontal cortex needs to be operating well. This area and others in the brain are best equipped to facilitate and guide us through this process.

4. There is a very powerful set of circuits in our brain, specifically our survival brain that developed many millions of years ago. The purpose of these circuits is to keep us safe. These safety messages are conveyed to us through fight, flight, and freeze mechanisms.

5. Whenever our human brain experiences fight, flight, or freeze responses, whether for one second or for years, our prefrontal cortex and related areas go relatively "offline."

6. Our ability to pursue reconnecting with our Essential Self becomes compromised.

Chapter 3

What Does Memory Have to Do with It?

I n the first few chapters, I hope you got some sense of what you want most, both at the surface (your initial answer), and deeper (your final answer), which is the one probably getting closer to your Essential Self. We also looked at where these qualities of the Essential Self are located on the big picture of Maslow's Hierarchy, which part of our human brain supports these highest levels of our actualization/transcendence, and what pulls these all important brain areas offline.

As interesting as this is, why should we care? Because this is our way back home.

Why should we care? Because this is our way back home.

Before we move on to better understand how we gradually stopped living through our Essential Self as children, let's first take a brief look at some of the different types of memory. This will make the material that follows easier to understand. Although there are many different types of memory, we're going to look at four that relate most to this book.

1. **Declarative Memory.** This type of memory is the most conscious that humans possess. Declarative memories are factual, without emotion, and they're usually pretty cut and dried. For example, if the material you are reading right now interests you, you may remember some of it later. You may not have any particular feelings attached to what you learned and recalled. This is simply factual information that you store in your brain as informational. It can be about people, events, places, etc., *but without emotion.* Another example of this could be my recall of some other items I want to include in this book. After I recalled them, I jotted them down in a list. There is no emotional charge or bodily reactivity in declarative memories. And again, these memories tend to be 100 percent conscious, meaning that you are fully aware of them.

   These memories tend to be stored in just a few parts of the brain, but mainly in the cortex, which, if you recall, is the outer layer of brain.

2. **Episodic Memory.** We are less consciously aware of this type of memory. While episodic memories are also factual, they can include emotions and the context of time, and other elements. Each of these elements comes from

different brain areas, but they all come together to create an actual event in our mind of what happened at some point in time. Our brain begins to create these episodic memories when we are about three-and-a-half years old. That's when our child-brain becomes capable of sequentially lining up the memories and the story of our life is thus created; this is when our *conscious awareness begins to become focused on this story, rather than the here-and-now reality of our lives.* Remember from before, our Essential Self is potentially accessed when we are in the "here and now," not the "there and then" of the story of our lives. Our Essential Self is a state of being, not a story or memory. So it is from about age three-and-a-half that our conscious awareness and attention gradually move from who we really are, to the "story of our life" that was created by a series of memories that tend to include elements of time and emotion.

> Our Essential Self is a state of being, not a story or memory.

You may wonder, "How is the story of my life different from the here and now?" First, we are moving from a state of being, the Essential Self, to a series of mental constructs, i.e., virtual memories. The first is 24 karat gold, while the second is fool's gold. The first is precious and authentic, the second appears to be valuable but is actually just a replica of our past experiences.

Research is finding that there is no such thing as a memory. Rather, there is a binding together of various perceptions, emotional reactions, sense of time, etc., which all come together temporarily to form what we think of as a memory. All of these pieces of input from various brain parts then break apart when you are no longer recalling the memory, until the next time you want to recall that memory.[3] So, in reality, a memory is a verb, not a noun.

Second, once this virtual memory process strongly takes hold from about age three-and-a-half on, our very creative brain accentuates whatever it has to in order to make the story of our lives hold together well. Our brain may weave a stronger emotional element throughout the story, even though it may not have been there.

These episodic memories involve many different brain areas, such as the thinking brain (prefrontal cortex), the emotional brain (the limbic areas), and many other brain areas. These work very closely together to integrate all of the pieces into one coherent creation of a memory. Again, nothing in this entire process includes our here-and-now state of being.

Nothing in this entire process includes our here-and-now state of being.

An example of a very negative episodic memory in my life was when my mother first hit me with great anger when I was a little over three years old. This was my first memory of how "bad and mean" my mother was. Before that incident, I would just flow with whatever was happening in our family. I didn't harbor negativity toward her, or anyone. Rather, I would be upset in the moment, but once the moment or incident passed, I was back to being in the now moment with her. However, when my brain matured enough to create episodic memories, this story was established in my mind. A part of the story included the strong emotions woven through it, and the recalled bodily sensations of the physical pain associated with it, and the nuances of the bodily and emotional sensations of loneliness after being hit. In other words, there was now a full-fledged story! That was when I first began to harbor fear and anger toward her. It then became easier and easier for my brain to add additional similar incidents over time to the "story" of my life.

Before we know it, our identity has quietly shifted from our state of being, the Essential Self, to the "story of our life."

An example of a positive series of episodic memories took place for me throughout my childhood, with a neighbor who lived across the street. Many of the children from our street would gather at Marian's house to play with her young children, but really to be around this wonderfully warm, loving, and kind woman. She had a way of making children feel valuable and loved, regardless of how they were treated in their own homes. This woman, and the story my brain created about her, helped sustain me through many childhood years.

Episodic memories are conscious, but they are connecting with other information that is not conscious, like emotions and bodily reactions, such as the emotional and bodily responses to the flight, fight, and freeze responses. Therefore, we're going deeper into brain areas that are evolutionarily older. The evolutionarily older the brain areas are, the more they tend to be unconscious and on autopilot.

Episodic memories can be guideposts in our lives, either positive or negative.

3. **Emotional Memory.** Now we are looking at memories that come from even deeper levels of our brain that are evolutionarily older. These are, as the term states, emotional. They come from deep within the unconscious brain. Now you may say, "But I am conscious and aware of when I feel emotions." While this is true, you are only consciously *noticing* the emotion with your thinking brain, the prefrontal cortex. Your thinking and noticing brain is not *creating* the emotion. Also, emotional memories are completely connected to our bodies. If you look closely the next time you feel any emotion, notice how you feel certain corresponding physical sensations in areas of your body, including the viscera (belly).

Emotional memories are completely connected to our bodies.

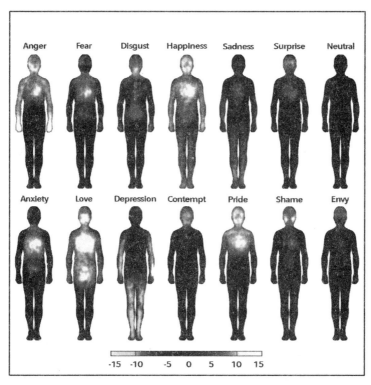

Figure 4: Emotional Bodily "Signatures"
(Nummenmaa, Glerean, Hari, & Hietanen, 2014)*

This is probably related to the evolution of emotions. A long time ago, emotions were initially generated to mobilize the ancient animals into certain kinds of action. For example, the emotions of fear and anger would mobilize their bodies into fleeing or fighting. Other emotions would mobilize them to seek food, shelter, a mate, protect their young, etc.

---

* Lauri Nummenmaa, Enrico Glerean, Riitta Hari, and Jari K. Hietanen, "Bodily Map of Emotions," *Proceedings of the National Academy of Sciences* 111, no. 2 (January 2014): 646-651, *http://doi:10.1073/pnas.1321664111.*

So it makes sense that the creation of our emotions is not from a conscious brain area. There was little conscious brain area when the emotion brain centers were first up and running millions of years ago.

Part of what determines the prominence of an emotional memory is the importance of the memory. For example, a young child will perceive its loving mother as extremely important. Therefore, memories of the mother will have high emotional charge, both positive and negative. The degree of charge is called *valence*.

4. **Procedural Memory:** Emotional memories are often closely tied together with this type of memory. Emotional memories can trigger procedural memories and vice versa. For example, a strong emotion of fear can trigger a flight response. The physical body is ready to run! When that flight response is triggered, we don't *think* about getting up, or telling our heart rate to increase, it's all happening on auto-pilot. That's an example of a procedural memory. There are similar procedural memories for anyone going into fight or freeze modes.

   Procedural memories are the most relevant to this book. They are rooted in the deeply unconscious areas of the brain, and involve recording, and then playing back sequences of actions and/or emotions that will run on autopilot whenever called forth to do so. Procedural memories can be very deeply locked into our brain, and difficult to change or erase.

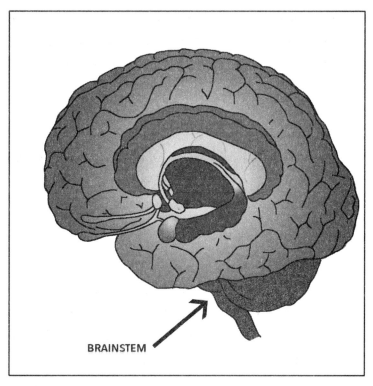

BRAINSTEM

**Figure 5: Brainstem: Origin of Many
Procedural Memories.**

Procedural memories can also be terrifically helpful to us. For example, after we learn to ride a bike, drive a car, or tie our shoelaces, our attention becomes freed up to focus on other things. Do you remember when you were first learning to drive a car? You had to pay very close attention to so many things, like stepping on the gas with the correct amount of pressure, not stopping too forcefully, estimating distances, passing cars, parallel parking, etc. But after some practice, you barely noticed how you were doing what you were doing. That's because your brainstem had taken the series of actions, strung them together and stored them away in your procedural memory brain files. Once there, much of it becomes unconscious.

Almost any action that you do repetitively may ultimately end up as a procedural memory.

One of the most common reasons our brain creates these procedural memories is to free up our conscious awareness and attention from activities that we do repetitively.

But these can also have a downside for us humans. What happens when a repetitive action becomes locked in as an unconscious procedural memory, but you really don't want it to, or you want it to stop as it is creating difficulties for you? Unfortunately, you may be stuck with it! Since the conscious mind has little to no connection or influence with this type of memory, it usually can't disassemble it. For example, your conscious mind is not capable of instructing your brainstem to unlearn how to drive a car, ride a bicycle, or tie your shoes. Short of actual brain injury or brain disease in these very specific brain areas, the procedural memory will usually remain.

Habits are another type of potentially helpful or unhelpful procedural memories. Luckily, most habits can be broken by retraining the brainstem over several weeks to months.

It is the procedural memories that involve survival responses, such as fight, flight, freeze, that tend to be the most difficult to break. Why would we even want to break a procedural memory that involves these responses since these are survival responses?

Because we all have many thousands of fight, flight, or freeze complexes that are locked together with non-threatening situations that are stored in our brain. They become reactivated, or triggered, every time we are reminded of the person or event. When we were children, our young and immature brains did not accurately understand the context of much of our experience. Our survival brain areas, by default, encoded them as potentially dangerous. These are specifically encoded as fight, flight, or freeze responses. This multitude of superfluous survival responses take up a significant percentage of our brain power, and severely limit our ability to be present in the here and now. Every time a fight, flight, or freeze response is activated, our prefrontal cortex goes relatively offline. Along with this, our connection with the "here and now" goes offline.

Another type of procedural memory is something I have seen very frequently. These are procedural memories that we unknowingly pick up from our parents or others that we are close to and spend a lot of time with, especially when we are children. These could be as simple as little mannerisms, like how we stand or laugh, all the way up to very complex behavioral patterns, attitudes, and the way we relate to ourselves and others.

An *introjection* is another type of procedural memory that becomes very deeply embedded in our unaware brain areas as children. This is a mechanism that all babies' and young children's brains utilize frequently by design. Babies and young children are wired to take in many of the qualities and attitudes of their caregivers, and possibly close siblings, as their own.

For example, as a mother and baby gaze into each other's eyes, the baby is downloading an enormous amount of unconscious information about itself through the mother. The mother's emotional state, attitudes about the baby, attitudes towards other people, are often taken in by the baby and about the baby. For example, if a mother is stressed and depressed, the baby may unconsciously take on the sense that there is something wrong with themselves. It's similar to downloading whole "screen shots" from a computer; it's as if the baby's actual identity is at least partially created by these introjections.

These "introjects" often become a part of the baby's unconscious and most basic framework of his or her core identity. Our very sense of who we are is heavily influenced by these early introjects. I like to refer to this phenomenon as the "scaffolding," "skeleton," or "background hum" of our identity. Like a software program, they are always running, but we are not aware of them unless we pay particular attention. These are some of the earliest elements of the development of our false self.

I also commonly see parents who consciously and/or unconsciously look down on one or more of their children. This could stem from the child reminding the parent of someone else they didn't like, a reaction related to the child's behavior, or a basic compatibility with the parent. Sharing genes doesn't always mean we are automatically a good fit. The point is, a young child may quickly introject that sense and live the rest of their life as if they are inferior. This is much more than just "feeling" one down. *The child, and eventually the adult he or she becomes, has*

*actually incorporated their most basic sense of self and identity
as being inherently inferior.* They can feel it deep down in their
bones. This is far more severe than just feeling one down or "less
than." This sense of inherent inferiority is always running, but
unless the person actually looks for it, they are generally not
even aware that it is there; again, it is part of the background
"hum."

Do we also introject positive aspects of our caregivers' attitudes, feelings, and behaviors toward us? Yes! We introject it
all—the good, the bad, and the ugly. Our baby brains are like
sponges with introjects; we soak up everything from our caregivers, with little to no screening or discernment.

That being said, once all of this information is introjected
into our brains and body (because remember, emotions are completely tied together with our physical bodies), the safety and
survival areas of the brain will pay much closer attention to the
negative introjects. The introjects that are positive and warm and
fuzzy are of little interest to our survival brain areas, although
they are very interesting and extremely important to other brain
areas for healthy emotional development and bonding.

But the survival brain areas take particular interest in the
negative introjects and begin to elaborate them into greater
complexity, i.e., the story of who we are, our worth, etc. Ultimately, since the survival brain areas can "scream" the loudest
in our brain and bodies, and thereby trump most other brain
circuits, it tends to be these negative introjects that cause us
problems down the line.

The final type of procedural memory that we will look at is closely related to one of the main themes of this book.

As described earlier, procedural memories are primarily related to the brainstem. A part of the brainstem contains the autonomic (pronounced auto-nom'-ic) nervous system. A lot of people mistake the word autonomic for the word automatic. Actually, this isn't that far from the truth, as the autonomic nervous system generally runs automatically, without our conscious control. The autonomic nervous system is what oversees our nervous system's basic level of excitability. For example, one extreme could be panic, all the way down to the other extreme, when we are deeply shut down and spaced out. Ideally, we usually want to be somewhere in the middle of the range. The bottom line is we want our baseline of excitability to be relaxed and calm, but attentive. Why? Because this is the zone that enables us to be in the here and now. This is typically the only state where we learn deep mastery in any given situation, and it is where we can access our Essential Self. When we are stuck being too amped up or too shut down at our baseline, our ability to reconnect with our Essential Self is decreased.

The bottom line is we want our baseline of excitability to be relaxed and calm, but attentive. Why? Because this is the zone that enables us to be in the here and now. This is typically the only state where we learn deep mastery in any given situation, and it is where we can access our Essential Self.

Our autonomic nervous system has two main branches: the sympathetic and parasympathetic nervous systems. The sympathetic branch (by the way, this has nothing to do with sympathy as in compassion for another person) is what drives us into increased excitability. This is the equivalent of stepping on the accelerator of a car. This is also the branch that can activate us into a fight or flight response. When it is too active, we can feel anxiety, panic, restlessness, hyperactive, belligerence and rage.

The parasympathetic branch of the autonomic nervous system is what calms and settles us down; it is like stepping on the brakes in a car. This is the branch of the nervous system that is most important when it comes to reclaiming and reconnecting with our Essential Self; this is the part of the nervous system that we most want to support and strengthen.

However, at the extreme, the parasympathetic nervous system can create a sense of depression, and leave us feeling shut down, disconnected, constricted, zoned out, and other symptoms that we'll look at later. These are freeze responses.

What does this have to do with procedural memories? These fight, flight, and freeze responses can become a type of procedural memory. When they become attached to various experiences, perceptions, and people in the brain, they become a very deep and unconscious form of procedural memory. I call these fight, flight, or freeze *complexes* (versus the unattached responses).

Once our brain attaches a fight, flight, or freeze response to anything that it perceives as a danger or a threat to our well-being, it will frequently stay attached. The accuracy of your brain's perception of danger is irrelevant. That means that for possibly years to come, every time your brain is reminded of this perceived threat or danger, that same fight, flight, or freeze response will become triggered. This works on autopilot. This also happens without your conscious awareness or consent. You may become consciously aware that your body and emotions are in a state of fight, flight, or freeze, but it's not your conscious awareness that has anything to do with the coupling of this response with a perception or experience of danger that you have. Remember, what your conscious mind considers dangerous, and what your ancient survival brain areas consider dangerous are often very different. They are each operating on software that are millions of versions apart. For example, millions of years ago, a large man wielding a stick and coming straight for you would have appropriately triggered a fight, flight, or freeze response. Jump ahead in time to modern man, where a boss raising his voice at you elicits that same fight, flight, or freeze response. Even though we are no longer in danger of imminent physical harm or death, our ancient survival brain areas are still generating a similar response. Another example: the parent of a young child becomes mildly depressed, the child's brain may perceive it as losing the parent and form a fight, flight, or freeze complex.

These fight, flight, or freeze complexes become stored deep in the brain, and have an extremely powerful ability to hijack us out of the here and now, and back into the fight, flight, or freeze responses of the there and then. What is going on in our brain at the moment of the hijacking is the activity in our brain shifting out of certain areas of the brain, usually in the outer shell, or cortex, and quickly back down to the ancient survival brain areas of the brainstem and limbic brain. Since these are unconscious areas of our brain, unlike the cortex, we have instantly vacated the here and now, and replaced it with a virtual memory. What does this have to do with the Essential Self? We can only be consciously connected to our Essential Self when we are in the present. But by their very nature, fight, flight, or freeze complexes hijack us out of the here and now of the brain cortex, and place us in the there and then of our ancient survival brain. This virtual "tape" of the physical and emotional equivalent of fight, flight, or freeze plays back to us. Subjectively, we experience the full-fledged fight, flight, freeze response in that moment, regardless of whether the threat is real. Nevertheless, it certainly *feels* real to us!

What happens to humans, more than any other species, is that our brain accumulates very large numbers of these fight, flight, or freeze complexes. Most other species have brains that process them through, or digest the tremendous energy associated with the creation of each of these fight, flight, or freeze responses or complexes. Therefore, the animal returns to its baseline functioning when the imminent danger is over. But we humans have an evolutionary glitch that leaves many of us with untold amounts of these complexes piling up over time. The accumulation can lead to all kinds of physical and emotional problems.

A now famous study was undertaken in the mid to late 1990's that addressed Adverse Childhood Experiences (ACE).[4] The results of this study revealed dramatic lifelong negative impact on our bodies and minds from ten different stressful experiences that many children encounter. The common element to all of these stressors is that they would likely generate significant amounts of chronic fight, flight, freeze reactions in children. The results demonstrated very significant medical, psychological, addictive, and socioeconomic problems that worsened for each additional item that someone had experienced before their eighteenth birthday. These problems could extend through our lifetimes.

Here are two case examples where we can apply some of these brain concepts.

David C. is a thirty-five-year-old sales representative who is about to either resign or get fired. He performs his job very well and had enjoyed it until his new manager came on board several months ago. This new boss is a "my-way-or-the-highway" kind of manager, and David often feels unappreciated and disrespected by him. David has thought that his boss was clearly wrong about some of his decisions and has vehemently argued with him several times. On one occasion, he became so angry he stormed out of the office, slamming doors behind him. David's coworkers also don't care much for the new manager, but they think David is overreacting. In the past, David had similar strong reactions to other authority figures: a Scout leader, a high school math teacher, and a team leader at an earlier job who ultimately fired him for insubordination.

Jane M. is a forty-seven-year-old, part-time clerical assistant for a real estate firm. She lives with her husband and youngest son, Alex, who is about to leave home for an out-of-state college. This will leave Jane and her husband in an empty nest. Her husband is sad to see Alex go, but welcomes the opportunity to have more time and space for himself. Jane had become quite depressed when the two older children left home, and is now more depressed than ever with Alex's impending departure. She slept only two to three hours each night, cried several times a day, had no energy, and lost her appetite as well as her interest in most things. She'd also had depressive episodes during her twenties whenever boyfriends would break up with her, and after her mother died several years ago.

David and Jane each experienced psychological traumas as children that their ancient survival brain areas interpreted as potential threats to their safety or well-being.

When David was five years old, his father became quite strict and demanding. David's young brain misinterpreted this and thought that his father was a threat to his survival. Out of the possible fight, flight, or freeze complexes available to his ancient survival brain areas, David's brain created a fight complex, which consisted of a fight response locked together with his father's angry demandingness and intimidation. Though he left home long ago, his brain still becomes triggered into fight mode whenever he feels unfairly challenged by an authority figure.

David has zero awareness that this fight, flight, freeze complex (in this case, a fight complex) has existed since childhood from interactions with his father. That is because all of this threat-survival circuitry is located within the brainstem and limbic brain areas that have no conscious awareness. With each incident of becoming angry or triggered by another authority figure in his life, David is only consciously aware of how unjust and pushy the other person is being. When he is triggered into the fight complex, he becomes angry, oppositional, and challenging. David has no conscious awareness that he is in a triggered fight state. All that he is consciously aware of is that his anger is justified by the situation.

He also becomes upset with his coworkers for not, in his words, "stepping up to the plate" by backing him up and joining him in confronting the manager. When they explain to him that they also don't like the manger, but that David's reaction to him is way out of line, he tells them they are just wimping out.

When Jane was two years old, her mother became moderately depressed after a close friend died. She was less emotionally available to Jane, and for a few months seemed sad much of the time. At that young age, Jane's immature thinking brain area, the prefrontal cortex, was too underdeveloped to understand the reality of her mother's situation. Jane's ancient survival brain areas interpreted that she was losing her mother, which for a two-year-old is extremely threatening—actually, about as terrifying as you can get at that age.

Her ancient survival brain areas generated a freeze response that became locked together with the perception of important people withdrawing from her. This then became an unconscious freeze complex, which may remain in her brain, ready to get triggered, for many years to come. This complex fires up whenever her survival brain areas perceive that someone important to her is withdrawing. She has no conscious awareness that this old complex is simply firing again; rather, she only has a *subjective* experience of feeling depressed and shut down (this is the freeze state). Her only conscious understanding comes from what her doctor tells her: that she has a chemical imbalance in her brain that leads to depression.

David and Jane are both demonstrating what happens when any one of our many, many stored up fight, flight, or freeze complexes become triggered, take over our emotional controls, and then run us on autopilot for at least a while. Some of these circuits only trigger us for moments, while others can lead us into a chronic state of fight (e.g., anger, aggression, oppositionality), flight (e.g., anxiety, panic, fear, restlessness), or freeze (e.g., feeling depressed, shutting down, spacing out, confusion, dissociating) for many years. This condition often becomes more complex as we develop layer upon layer of chronic fight, flight, and/or freeze. *For every additional complex that becomes stored within our brain, we lose that much more access to our true self.*

Jane's and David's autopilot reactions demonstrate a type of procedural memory. Remember that fight, flight, or freeze responses are not memories at all. Rather, they are normal survival-based responses. However, when this response becomes locked together with something else, like an intimidating father, or mother who disconnects from you, or a dog that bites you, it then becomes a fight, flight, or freeze complex, which also act as procedural memories.

We can become triggered from current and/or old perceived threats or dangers, real or unreal. When left in a state of chronic fight, flight, or freeze reactions, we are chronically more challenged to access our Essential Self. Since most of us have an abundance of these complexes, it becomes increasingly challenging to access our Essential Self.

We will be revisiting some of these points throughout the book, because as you can see they are extremely important for understanding why we lose so much conscious connection with our Essential Self.

Key Points

1. We reviewed four types of memories. Each type originates from increasingly deep brain levels. The deeper a brain level is, the less conscious it is.

2. The memories that are generated from the deepest brain levels are unconscious, and are typically manifested in bodily and emotional expressions.

3. Since they are unconscious, they can weave together seamlessly with our conscious mind, and often we have no conscious awareness that they are present. They feel like the "here and now," but they are actually the "there and then" playing back.

Chapter 4

More on the Essential Self

Now, let's take the next step! How did we get from living as our Essential Self when we were young children to where we are right now, which for most folks is very disconnected from the Essential Self? In terms of Maslow's hierarchy, how did we get thrown off track in the progression toward what we want most, which is at the top of the pyramid?

We are born with our Essential Self and our identity as one and the same. However, we have no ability for self-reflection as very young children. Therefore, we don't have any awareness that these are one and the same. As our brain's ancient survival mechanisms create powerful and uncomfortable fight, flight, and freeze responses that

> *We are born with our Essential Self and our identity as one and the same. However, we have no ability for self-reflection as very young children. Therefore, we don't have any awareness that these are one and the same.*

babies and young children are powerless to control, the peaceful Essential Self is increasingly forgotten. Our identity and Essential Self are no longer one and the same.

Our identity shifts from our Essential Self to the physical body of a baby and young child that completely depends on their caregivers to buffer them from having fight, flight, freeze reactions, and to calm and soothe them when they do have them. This is how children ultimately learn to regulate their emotions. But in the meantime, their Essential Self and identity are no longer one and the same.

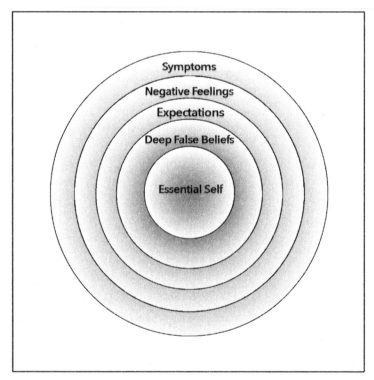

Figure 6A: The Layers That Cover Our Essential Self.

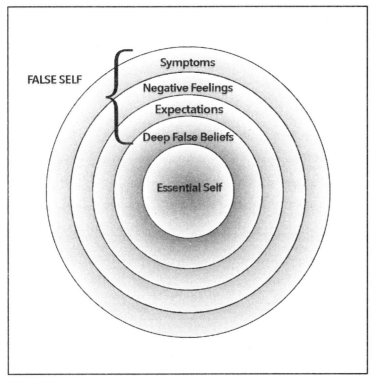

Figure 6B: The False Self.

When we are a little older, our thinking brain (the prefrontal cortex) has matured a bit more, and this enables us to think and understand more deeply and clearly. Because of this, we are better able to buffer ourselves from fight, flight, and freeze responses. One of the ways we do this is by creating Deep False Beliefs. This is represented in the second circle of the diagram. These Deep False Beliefs are a young child's attempts at curbing the frequency of having these fight, flight, and freeze responses triggered. These Deep False Beliefs are a product of the child's immature understanding of who they should be in order to keep their parents happy and thereby maintaining a sense of security and equilibrium. There are potentially an unlimited number and variety of Deep False Beliefs that a child's brain can create, and most first graders that I have met already have thousands of them!

The next few chapters will look at each circle of the diagram more carefully. For now, we'll take a general snapshot of each layer of circles.

The next circle represents the *expectations* that we create from these Deep False Beliefs. Each of these erroneous beliefs can have from a few to a multitude of expectations that are offshoots. For example, there may be an infinite number of expectations from just the one Deep False Belief, such as: "Whatever I do, I better do well!" A few of these expectations could be: "I have to make good grades," or "I have to do well at sports," or "I have to dress right."

We will go into more detail later, but for now just know that each Deep False Belief is attached to a fight, flight, or freeze response. Is this a fight/flight/freeze *complex*? Yes. It is the belief's attachment to a fight, flight, or freeze response that sets it apart from other beliefs and gives it such a powerful emotional charge!

As our brain becomes cluttered with so many Deep False Beliefs and expectations of ourselves and others, we turn farther and farther away from our Essential Self. We become increasingly attached to the "story" of who we are, our relationships with others, how we perform at school, sports, excelling at different things, trying to make our parents proud of us, fitting in with our peers, and so forth. Is there anything inherently wrong with any of this?

No, but there will be no deep and long-lasting peace until we retrieve the true self we left behind. *The more we turn away from our Essential Self, the more symptomatic we become and the more we suffer.* By midlife, most of us have a gnawing sense that there is something more to life that we just can't put our finger on ... well, this is it!

Here are some additional points about the Essential Self that integrate some very important brain information.

"Shoulds" Versus the Real Thing

Even though we touched on this in the first exercise, this is so important I want to say more about it. When we consider some of the inherent qualities of the Essential Self—such as peace, deep happiness, a sense of freedom, a sense of unity, and love— it's important to remember that we should not *act* like we are those qualities. If we were to do so, it would mean living from a list of "shoulds," as we discussed earlier.

When we are simply *being* our Essential Self, these inherent qualities are effortlessly manifested by us. They are non-conceptual and timeless; they are more of a state of "is-ness" than "doing-ness." Also, they don't require any thought. If anything, our thoughts can get in the way! They are our selves, who and what we are—the most real. These qualities transcend deeper than the thinking and emotions of our day-to-day lives.

Think about that for a moment. Do you ever catch yourself thinking, *Oh, this is how I should be feeling, thinking, or acting?*

Notice how different that feels than when you experience these qualities just flowing through you, without any effort. Here is a simple exercise to help you gain greater clarity about the difference:

List five examples of "shoulds" that often influence how you think, behave, and relate to others. Before you begin writing, consider some of the more subtle ways "shoulds" influence you in addition to the obvious ones you already know about.

1. _____

_____

2. _____

_____

3. _____

_____

4. _____

_____

5. _____

_____

Our ability to attune to and align with our Essential Self is of paramount importance.

Knowing who we really are is probably the most important task of our lives. It's the Essential Self that can lead us to the best paths and choices to make. When our identity becomes aligned with the wisdom and knowingness of the Essential Self, it becomes a valuable life compass. It's also

Knowing who we really are is probably the most important task of our lives.

inherently gratifying when we are living as our Essential Self because we are *home*. This feels so much better than living from the survival-based—which are really fear-based—brain areas that create so many conditioned behaviors and attitudes that become integrated into our personalities. Additionally, when we reclaim and reconnect with our Essential Self, it is analogous to being deep in the ocean: the surface waves and turbulence just don't touch us.

Inside the Brain

In order to make all of this clearer, let's take a look at what's happening in the brain. First, there are two brain concepts that may give you a better understanding of the big picture:

Concept One

The smallest building blocks of what drive our attention away from our Essential Self are the fight, flight, and freeze brain responses or complexes that we have alluded to a few times. Once you understand these, everything else that follows will make much more sense. In a very similar vein, the same brain areas can attach emotional "charges" to people, situations, and experiences that it deems as important. These may not be actual fight, flight, or freeze responses, but rather varying degrees of emotional charges. As mentioned earlier, this is called "emotional valence."

As stated earlier, the Essential Self is a state of being; it is not a thought, concept, or belief. We are either tuned into the state of being, or not; similar to turning the dial on a radio. When we are not tuned in, we are wide open to the "loud" influences of the flight, fight, and freeze responses and strong emotions, which are analogous to radio static. They are so loud because nature and evolution intended them to immediately grab 100 percent of our attention, and move us into fleeing, or fighting, or freezing. But they also block out the quiet whisper of the Essential Self.

Our Deep False Beliefs, and offshoot expectations, are most commonly manifested as the day-to-day and moment-to-moment thoughts, inner dialogue, or commentary that we have constantly running through our heads. If you examine these thoughts more closely, you'll see that most of them are ultimately tied in to some type of survival-related fight, flight, freeze complex, or strong emotions. For example, I once spent an entire day, with pen and notebook in hand, recording every thought that crossed my mind. What I first noticed was that my thoughts are amazingly boring and horrifically repetitive. But when I analyzed each one, I found that almost each and every thought, when traced back to its origin, was the product of thinking that *there is something I need to think, say, or do in order to fit in, or get someone's approval, or play it safe, or be a good, acceptable person.* These are examples of thoughts that are generated from survival beliefs.

Here is an example of a more blatant survival-based experience: If you are sitting quietly at home reading, and all of a sudden there is a thunderously loud *BOOM!* right outside your window, chances are you're going to drop whatever you are reading, no matter how fascinating, and run to the window to see what is happening. This is called an *orienting* response. This is when our brain quickly figures out if we are in danger, to what degree we are in danger, and what we should do next. During those moments of orienting, both our ancient survival brain areas and our modern thinking brain areas are checking in with the hippocampus. This is the extremely complex filing system of our brain that we looked at in an earlier chapter in relation to episodic memory. In an instant, it can sort through millions of "files" of past experiences and quickly assess the degree of danger.

What is concurrently going on in our brain and body is that a specific part of the ancient survival brain area, the amygdala, instantly fired a signal to the physically lowest and evolutionarily oldest part of the brain, the brainstem, instructing it to fire the electrical, chemical, and hormonal responses that instantly put the body and brain on high alert. The body is now ready to run away (flight), or protect or challenge (fight). If these fail, and we perceive we are powerless to escape or protect, the next brain signal is for shutting down, or entering freeze mode, which originates from a different area of the brainstem. Chronic fight and flight reactions can lead to chronically *overactive* ancient survival brain areas, and chronic freeze reactions can lead to chronically *underactive* areas of the brain.

Ancient survival responses are engineered and designed to get our attention until we are relatively safe. We would not stop in the middle of one of these emergency responses and think *Hmm, I wonder how my Essential Self is doing?* When the fight, flight, and/or freeze responses are activated, almost all of our thinking and reflecting parts of the brain, many of which are in the evolutionarily newest brain areas of the prefrontal cortex, come to a crashing halt.

When we are young children, our thinking and analyzing brain areas are still too immature to understand or form concepts about what is happening. Also, the hippocampus doesn't yet have many files of experience. During that orienting phase, young children have an inadequate buffering system in place. There is nothing buffering or preventing the amygdala from firing away with fight, flight, and/or freeze responses to just about anything. As mentioned earlier, young children's brains are partially buffered by their caregivers protecting them. But there remains a multitude of jarring and unnecessary brain responses that overwhelm children's survival brain circuits, emotions, and bodies.

Adults' brains are able to prevent many potential fight, flight, freeze-complex firings, as areas of our thinking brains and hippocampus have a much greater understanding as to what constitutes a danger and what does not. Adults can modulate, to some degree, how much their amygdalae fire the fight, flight, and/or freeze response.

The net result is young children are extremely vulnerable to the frequent firing of these survival-driven responses, and gradually become disconnected from the Essential Self state of being. As children turn away from experiencing and living the inherent qualities of the Essential Self, their lives gradually give way to living as the false self. (Even though adults are able to discern and not take on as many new fight, flight, freeze complexes as young, inexperienced children, the adult brain already has loads of these complexes stored from childhood. These do not usually go away on their own.)

Concept Two

Let's step up to a bigger picture to see what a developing child's brain does with these fight, flight, and/or freeze responses and complexes, which also play a major role in forcing the child's attention away from the Essential Self.

At Approximately Three Months Old

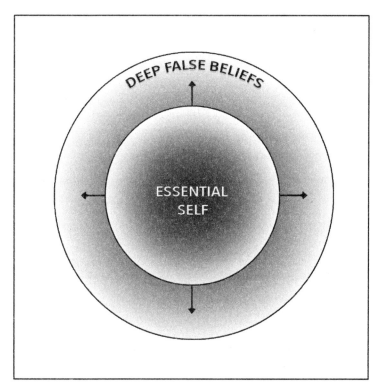

Figure 7: At Approximately Three Months Old, We Begin Developing Early Forms of Deep False Beliefs. This Is the Result of the Dawning "Me" Sense Interfering with Our Connection with Our Essential Self.

At about three months of age, many children experience their first dawning awareness that there is a *me*. Before that, we are cognizant of others and are aware of interacting with them, but have no real conscious awareness that there is a *separate* me.

Even though this me sense is still quite rudimentary at the tender age of three months, it is nonetheless a huge wake-up call for the ancient survival parts of the brain. Now that our survival brain recognizes that there is a me who is a completely vulnerable infant and is wholly dependent upon a few people, this part of our brain has a heyday as it recognizes that it must protect this newly identified person from any perceived or potential harm. Now that there is an individual to protect, these survival brain areas become much more active. These brain areas over-interpret many things as potentially dangerous.

An analogy would be a dog whose behavior differs when his family is away versus when they are home. Consider this example from my childhood.

When I was growing up, our family dog, Boris, had this pattern: if no one was home and he was in our backyard, a neighbor could throw a treat over the fence, and Boris would welcome them through the gate and into the yard with open paws. If dogs could speak, I imagine him saying, "Oh, thank you for the wonderful and delicious treat! Come on into the yard and then help yourself to anything you'd like in the house."

This same dog was completely different when we were home. He would bark and growl at passersby, serving as our valiant protector.

Our survival brain areas act much the same as Boris did once there is a person to protect.

These fight, flight, and/or freeze responses are very uncomfortable for children, more so than for adults. They can't get up and run away, or fight to protect themselves. They also can't figure out the larger context of the situation. Their little bodies become flooded with powerful chemicals, stress hormones, and overpowering emotions generated by the flight, flight, freeze responses. Yet, they are powerless can do almost nothing to better their circumstances.

There are strong emotions that are generated from the fight, flight, and/or freeze responses or complexes, for example, fear from the flight response, anger from the fight response, and sadness, shame, guilt, despondency, and shutting down from the freeze response. As we saw earlier, our human bodies always respond to any emotions we are having, and emotions and their bodily responses work together as one unit.

Emotions and their bodily responses work together as one unit.

Therefore, these very uncomfortable bodily and emotional responses to the fight, flight, freeze responses and complexes also grab the child's attention and turn it away from the subtle Essential Self.

How does this dawning sense of me translate to the experience of a three-to-six-month-old child? Their moment-to-moment experience is beginning to rest in the sense of "me," instead of the state-of-being that has no identification or limits.

At Approximately Six Months Old

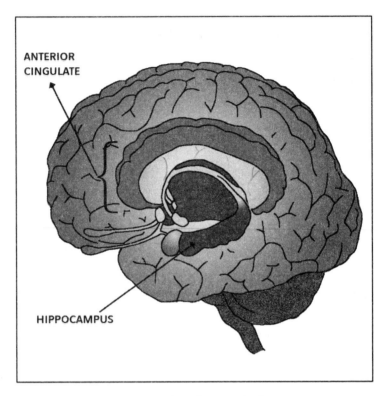

Figure 8: Anterior Cingulate and Hippocampus.
These Impact Our Connection with the Essential Self.

The anterior cingulate is a brain area that sits between that modern thinking brain, the prefrontal cortex, and part of the ancient survival brain area that partly generates the intense emotions. Don't worry about the name; all that is important is to understand that at approximately six months old, many babies' brains have matured enough that this part of their brain can now take over from their caregivers in comforting themselves from strong emotions and the physical counterparts. They now have greater capacity for what is referred to as better self-regulation of their emotional states.

How does this tie in with the Essential Self? In order for young children to successfully transition into this gradually improving self-regulation, the bonding and attachment with their caregivers grows increasingly strong and complex. They slowly increase the mastery of their emotions through the ongoing and repeated calming from their caregivers.

This, as you can see, increasingly pulls their attention in the direction of their parents, and the world outside of themselves. The Essential Self becomes less and less a part of children's daily lives.

Three-and-a-Half Years Old

Let's go back to a part of the brain we looked at a little earlier that controls certain types of memory: the hippocampus. At around age three and a half, the hippocampus is beginning to do its job as the giant file cabinet and storywriter, and shares this information between the thinking brain and the emotional brain. This is a critically important timeframe, as our entire experience of life takes a giant step away from the Essential Self, and locks into the life-story that is now more fully created. Past, present, and future are now seamlessly integrated into the story, as well as all kinds of positive and negative emotions. Overall, the hippocampus turns us away from our simple here and now experience of the Essential Self, toward a richly textured story, with emotions woven tightly throughout. We are now living fully within the "there and then" and future projections. All of this is influenced by the ancient survival brain. This is a giant step forward into our identifying as the false self.

At this tender age, our own mind is now capable of triggering these fight, flight, and/or freeze responses/complexes over and over again. In many respects, our own thinking now has the potential to become our worst enemy.

We now have the potential to dwell on the past and get stuck in it. This opens up a whole additional can of worms as, at this tender age, *our own mind* is now capable of triggering these fight, flight, and/or freeze responses/complexes over and over again. In many respects, our own thinking now has the potential to become our worst enemy.

Our inner stories are also heavily weighted in the direction of negativity, as that is what the ancient survival brain areas are most interested in. For example, these brain areas are far more interested in Mommy or Daddy getting upset with us than when they smile at us and are happy with us, because it doesn't weigh in as being a potential threat or danger. As described earlier, other brain areas are very interested in our bonding with our caregivers, but not these powerful fight, flight, or freeze circuits.

As our life story evolves and becomes more complex over time, our conscious attention becomes more firmly rooted in our false self, and moves farther and farther away from our Essential Self.

Approximately Ages Seven to Nine Years

By the time they are seven to nine years old, children's brains are developing what is called the *Default Mode Network (DMN)*. The relevant point here is that children at this age have now developed a sense of "me" that remains consistent and present whenever they are not engaged in an activity. That is, that sense of me is now their default mode of experiencing themselves most of the time.

For example, if you compare a two-year-old with a nine-year-old, the two-year-old will naturally default to the state of being of the Essential Self. But when we consider a nine-year-old, their attention will default to their sense of "me"—that is, their thoughts, emotions, and/or body; i.e., the false self.

This makes reconnecting with our Essential Self even more challenging.

Before we move on, let me share with you my very first memory. My earliest awareness of the Essential Self came when I was a very young child. This experience strongly captured my attention and has remained with me ever since. I was seeing images that I eventually came to understand were faces. They were all looking in one direction. Ultimately, I became aware that what they were looking at was *me*. It was the first time I had awareness that I existed. The most important part of this memory was the *timeframe before* I became aware of *me*. There was a timeless, expansive, and peaceful sense, and nothing was separate from that. The moment I had an awareness of a me, this all collapsed into the far more limited and constricted sense of me as a little body that was uncomfortable.

I never forgot the true nature that underlies my personality, attitudes, strengths, and weaknesses. This led to a whole other quality of existence. With the dawning realization of myself as my own little person, my consciousness went from connectedness and peace, to the serious business of living and surviving.

Key Points

1. "Shoulds" versus the real thing: When we think or behave from a "should," that is typically the voice of our thinking mind, e.g., *I should smile, I should be kind,* etc. This can be a good thing, but it is very different from when the qualities of the Essential Self issue forth automatically, simply because these qualities are a natural part of who we are.

2. The importance of tuning in to our Essential Self: Our culture has not typically recognized or understood the Essential Self; rather, it only understands and values the mind and its voluminous numbers of thoughts. Most people in our culture do not come to recognize the Essential Self until they are dying or are in a life-threatening or other serious event. The Essential Self is the most real and genuine part of us. We can't afford to ignore it; the price is too high. This causes us to abandon who we are at our core.

3. Much of humankind's current survival brain areas are similar to those from many millions of years ago. Mankind's sophisticated thinking brain, the prefrontal cortex, was not around back then; it had not yet evolved. So the current default connections between these two parts of the brain are not very strong. Therefore, our ancient survival brain areas are still operating in the dark, as if we are still cavemen with little sophisticated thinking and understanding

ability. However, areas of the brain cortex can train and buffer these ancient survival brain areas.

4. Despite its being significantly out of tune with the lives of modern man, our ancient survival brain areas possess the most powerful brain circuitry. These can easily over-power any of the functions of our thinking brain. This translates to our attention and focus going in the direction of where the real charge or "loud voice" is, most which is often from the ancient survival brain areas, with its fight, flight, and freeze responses, and/or attaching increased emotional valence.

5. If left unchecked, the ancient survival brain areas will over-power other brain circuits. Later in this book, we will look at how to combat this tendency.

6. The smallest unit of how the ancient survival brain areas can operate is through generating a fight, flight, and/or freeze response. When our limbic brain and brainstem fire off a flight response, our body and emotions instantly go into fear, anxiety, panic, and restlessness, etc. When a fight response is triggered, our body and emotions go into anger, frustration, oppositionality, irritability, and aggres-siveness, etc. And when a freeze response is generated, our bodies and emotions constrict and shut down; we can feel "spacey" or faint, depressed, and/or powerless.

7. When any of the three are triggered, our thinking brain goes offline. This means that our thinking, analyzing and understanding faculties are not fully available to us when we are in a fight, or flight, and/or freeze response. These are the times we need them most!

8. For young children, who naturally have very little prefrontal cortex functioning, and very little adaptive hippocampus functioning the ancient survival fight, flight, freeze responses are often overpowering to their functioning and psychological development. Their young brains do their best to mitigate these responses. One of these ways is by creating Deep False Beliefs. But their personalities have to grow through and around the fight, flight, freeze complexes, and their Deep False Beliefs, which typically number in the thousands by the time children start school.

9. Episodic memories are tied together by the hippocampus to create the story of our lives, beginning at approximately age three-and-a-half. The more our life story grows, the more we abandon the here and now, and therefore, our Essential Self.

10. Procedural memories of the fight, flight, or freeze complexes begin to pile up when we are still children. When any of these are activated, they hijack us out of the here and now and drop us into the there and then.

Yet we believe we are still in the here and now, as these triggered complexes are virtual memories and feel very real. It is very difficult to access our Essential Self when we are in the there and then.

Principles of Essential Living

- *At a young age, the human brain turns its attention away from our Essential Self and toward our outer world.*

- *As a child, our mind, which is mainly a product of the survival brain programming, becomes fascinated with our outside world. It is far more intensely emotionally charged, both positive and negative, than our Essential Self's quiet state of being. We become captivated by our outside world and our mind loves this.*

- *We lose conscious connection with our Essential Self. We forget who we are. We begin to suffer. This is caused by an evolutionary glitch.*

Chapter 5

Deep False Beliefs: One of the Underpinnings of Our False Self

The fight, flight, and freeze responses that we have been looking at are normal, transient, and are typical brain responses to a perceived threat or danger, whether accurate or inaccurate. They become activated in the ancient survival parts of our brain and put our body and emotions on high alert. This is followed by the body and emotions returning to their baseline when the alert signal is over. Most people experience these responses fairly often to varying degrees of intensity. For example, it can happen when a driver honks his horn at you, in the moment you realize someone is standing right behind you, when you receive a letter with an IRS return address, or hear the total amount you owe at the Whole Foods checkout counter.

Your body and emotions go into fear, anger, or shut-down mode. You return to normal when your brain knows you are safe.

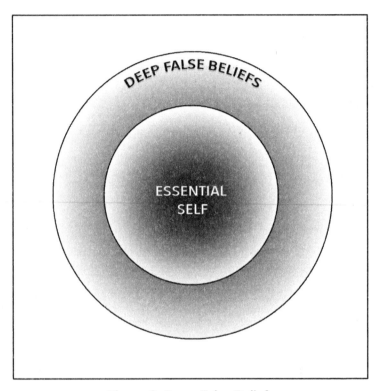

Figure 9: Deep False Beliefs

We also looked at what happens when one of these usual fight, flight, or freeze responses becomes locked together with a *specific* perception, experience, person, or belief—when it goes from being a simple fight, flight, or freeze response—to what I call a *complex*. This means that whichever perception, experience, person, or belief that has been locked together with a fight, flight, and freeze response, it has the potential to be triggered or retriggered. Whenever one of these complexes is created, it is usually stored in the brain, ready to fire whenever you are reminded of that perception, experience, person, belief, etc. This potential triggering can remain in your brain for many years.

From a previous example, when Jane's mother withdrew from her when she was two years old, Jane's survival brain areas locked together a freeze response with the experience of someone important withdrawing from her. So every time Jane perceives someone important withdrawing from her, the "freeze response + person leaving" complex becomes retriggered, and another bout of sadness and depression is precipitated. (By the way, I am *not* saying that all cases of depression are caused by a freeze response. Rather, that many cases of chronic freeze states may present themselves as depressions. There are many other causes of depression.)

Also from a previous example, when David was five years old, and his father became quite authoritarian and angry with him during power struggles, David's survival brain areas locked together a fight response with the perception of someone unjustly wielding power over him. This became a "fight + authoritarian-person" complex. This can become retriggered whenever he is involved with an authoritarian figure.

Here's another example: Chelsea, a twenty-eight-year-old woman I treated, had been raped by a man wearing a blue shirt. She developed panic attacks (flight), which occurred whenever she saw any man in a blue shirt. This means her brain contains a complex that is made up of a flight response that is locked together with men wearing blue shirts. When she sees a man with this color shirt, the flight response becomes triggered, and she becomes panicked and anxious.

I want to share one more example that clearly shows how independent this response is from our conscious thinking, which is in the prefrontal cortex, not the ancient survival brain areas. A number of years ago, I was working at a hospital that hired an executive director, William, who was quite unfriendly and at times cruel to the staff. It took about a year for the hospital to fire him.

During that year, a woman named Stacey worked directly under William, and carried out many of his threats and staff firings. The two of them acting together made for a very unpleasant work environment.

A few years after Stacey had stopped working at this hospital, I was attending a psychiatric conference in a different part of the country. As I sat in the large hotel ballroom at the opening of the event, I saw a woman sitting diagonally across from me, in an aisle seat, whose hair looked almost identical to Stacey's. Immediately, my heart began to race. I felt the blood quickly coursing through my arteries, and I was almost numb with fear. The woman turned around and I saw her face. I was relieved to see she was not Stacey, and in fact had no resemblance to her other than the hairstyle. My body and emotions calmed down.

A few minutes later, when the back of this woman's head was facing me again, and I saw the same type of hair and style that Stacey had, my heart began to instantly race again, and I momentarily felt strong fear and panic. But this time, there was a calm center within me and I was fully conscious that this woman was not Stacey. As odd as it might sound, it happened a few more times despite the fact that I knew full well that Stacey was not there. Finally, the autopilot triggering into flight mode from seeing hair that resembled Stacey's came to a stop. That is, my survival brain areas finally understood that this was not anyone who was going to threaten me. Notice how my thinking brain and survival brain areas each had a life of their own.

What does all of this brain stuff have to do with Deep False Beliefs? They are one type of fight, fight, or freeze complex, which are generally created when we are children when a belief becomes attached to fight, flight, or freeze response.

These Deep False Beliefs are very different from most of the rules or beliefs we create or adopt in our teen or adult years, such as when we say, "It's Wednesday, so I need to take out the garbage," or "I believe that the best way to invest my money is in mutual funds." The rules and beliefs that we adopt as adults are generally not tightly bound together with survival-based fight, flight, or freeze responses! We don't become deeply triggered into these responses with these kinds of rules, because most of the rules we create as adults are not related to our most basic survival wiring.

Deep False Beliefs can exist in layers, which can make some of the deeper layers very subtle. For example, when my siblings and I were young, my mother's unspoken message about my older brother was that he was the most important of the six children. Implicit within that message was that the other five children were less important. Did anyone ever say that? No. But was it a powerful message regardless? Yes! This became deeply embedded in my psyche, and has reared its head through many different situations over the years.

In a related vein, since the majority of our Deep False Beliefs were created as children, our personalities, coping styles, and skills, develop through and around these complexes throughout our formative years.

These types of hidden or masked unspoken Deep False Beliefs run rampant in our brains! Many cultures and families express a preference for boys or girls. For example, in areas of China and India, sons have been historically preferred over daughters. This frequently created a belief in the "chosen" children that they had a lot to live up to, but at a more subtle level, the other children bought into a "second-best" valuation of themselves. We refer to this as feeling "one down," or "disempowered."

We all have thousands of Deep False Beliefs that are of a wide variety, and affect many different areas of our lives.

When we were young children and our survival brain areas were triggering the fight, flight, freeze responses, we'd be left feeling physically and emotionally uncomfortable. These responses are very stressful on the body and our emotional state. And remember that babies and young children are not capable of fleeing or fighting in response to the massive chemical, hormonal, and electrical stimulation of the fight, flight, freeze complexes. This condition of learned helplessness can leave us in states of chronic stress and a pervasive sense of powerlessness, which can continue long after the stresses end. It is the caregiver's role to buffer young children from being exposed to events, people, and parental emotions/behaviors that overly stress young children, but this potential protection is far from perfect in human cultures. As young children, since we are not yet physically capable of fleeing or fighting, our young child brain does its best to minimize the impact of these responses.

One of the ways is it tries to figure out the "rules of life" and how to work with them as best as possible. Keep in mind, young children have very immature thinking brains that understand very little about the reality of the people and world around them. The rules that they figure out tend to be inaccurate and very rigid, as that is the way young children think. Regardless, these Deep False Beliefs that they create remain locked in their brain and can become triggered at any age.

The most important thing to a young child is keeping his or her emotional and physical connection with their parents and/or other caregivers who are important to them. Their survival brain areas know for certain that maintaining these relationships is the most important thing for survival. The primary goal of these "rules of life" is to maintain important connections with the parents while, at the same time, minimizing exposure to the very uncomfortable fight, flight, and freeze responses.

The primary goal of these "rules of life" is to maintain important connections with the parents while, at the same time, minimizing exposure to the very uncomfortable fight, flight, and freeze responses.

A few examples of some of the more common Deep False Beliefs include:

Life should be fair! (This is a deep one and very common.)

Getting angry is unsafe; I may lose Mommy and Daddy's love.

I have to be really good to be lovable.

Whatever I do, I better do well.

Whatever I do, I better do perfectly.

I must keep Mommy and Daddy happy with me, or else I
will lose their love.

I am not as valuable as _____.

I shouldn't cry too much, or Mommy and Daddy won't
love me and then I'll be in trouble.

I am bad if I get angry (and if I'm bad, Mommy and Daddy
won't love me, and then . . . uh-oh!).

I should be nice to other people—or else!

I'm not good enough.

I'm not worthy.

Unless I am _____, I just won't measure up.

Unless I do _____, I just won't measure up.

Remember Jane and David? Jane's survival brain and thinking brain created a Deep False Belief that went something like this: *No matter how good I am, I'm not good enough for my mommy to love me.* (Remember, her mother became depressed when Jane was two years old.)

David's Deep False Belief went something like this: "Authority figures will harm you."

Deep False Beliefs are often subtle and hidden. The earlier they were created in our lives, the more subtle they tend to be. These subtle ones tend to operate in the "background hum" of our daily lives, away from our conscious awareness. They are part of the background scaffolding of how we experience ourselves, others, and the world around us. For example, when I was a young child, my brain created the belief that adults know better than me so I should always defer to them. This wasn't something I would sit down and ponder. Instead, I just automatically assumed it to be true.

As you can guess, the Deep False Beliefs that our mind created as very young children tend to be quite powerful. In fact, they very often run the show without our being aware of it.

Another example took place with a good friend of mine named Stephanie. She described that during her preteen and early teen years, her father would have to drive her to the library to use reference books for schoolwork. He would come into the library with her, sit close by, fold his hands, and do nothing but wait for her. He did not even unbutton his heavy winter coat or remove his scarf and hat, even though it was warm inside. Stephanie would feel quite anxious to get her work done as quickly as possible, so her father wouldn't have to wait long. The thought that repeatedly went through her mind was: *I'm taking too long!* and she would feel sick to her stomach. Although considerable time has passed since then, when someone has to wait for her, Stephanie feels very anxious and nauseous. The subtle but erroneous belief that her preteen brain created went something like: *I am not worthy of having someone wait for me.*

How much of this is usually conscious? Very little. In Stephanie's case, during the past thirty-five years, her experience when someone is waiting for her is mainly a subjective sense of high anxiety and stomach disturbance, and as she described, the recurrent thought that she is taking too long.

When children reach school age, the brain has matured to the point where peer relationships become front and center in terms of importance. This is a remaining vestige from eons ago, when breaking away from the pack meant certain death. Safety was found in numbers. Mankind still has that deeply encoded in the survival brain. Caregivers are still important, but not being singled out from the pack has become more important. This can be borne out from our own experience.

Think back to your elementary, junior, or high school years. Try to recall a very painful experience. Does recalling it still make you cringe inside, even today? That inner cringing is the bodily, specifically visceral response to a fight, flight, or freeze complex that's been stored in our brain for a long time. For now, just realize that the cringing is this fight, flight, or freeze response that was bound together with whatever the memory was. This means that when you think of that old experience, you are right back in the discomfort of it; even if it was many years ago and presently has zero relevance to your life. Similarly, your cognitive (prefrontal cortex) understanding of it now, and the realization (prefrontal cortex) of how "that was then and now is now" will make absolutely no difference in preventing the memory from triggering the same fight, flight, or freeze response. This applies to either now or in the future. Again, when triggered, this response seamlessly weaves together with your current experience, so you don't know that you have been hijacked out of the here and now.

There are potentially an unlimited number of Deep False Beliefs; i.e., whatever a person's brain *thinks* is a rule for maintaining their parents' love, or from standing out in a negative way from our peers, etc.

Children's brains physically mature as they progress through childhood. As they do, they become increasingly capable of more accurate and complex thinking and understanding. Therefore, the Deep False Beliefs of a two-year-old and a six-year-old, tend to be very different. Items on the list (on page 102) would actually apply to children of all different ages.

Let's take a schematic look, using Figure 10 on the following page, at how these "old tapes" play out when we are triggered. You are the person on your right. In A, you are responding to the other person in the "here and now." In B, you are "triggered" and an old tape plays seamlessly with your current experience. You respond to the other person as if you are in the here and now, but you are not.

Regardless of what age the Deep False Belief was created, it will still play back to us the exact same message, regardless of how old we become. For example, the Deep False Belief that *I shouldn't get angry* often develops when a child is young and becomes very angry about someone or something. This is a totally normal childhood reaction.

When most young children feel raw anger or rage, their parents naturally want to quash it. But when the child sees the negative facial expression or feels the negative reaction of their psychologically important parents, the child may instantly and instinctively go into a fight, flight, or freeze reaction. They may feel shame, which can be a manifestation of a freeze response. After several experiences like this, in order to avoid the powerful physical and emotional experience of seeing their unhappy parents, the child's relatively undeveloped thinking brain will create a Deep False Belief that goes something like *Uh-oh, Mom and Dad may not love me if I get angry. I better stop it or I might lose their love.*

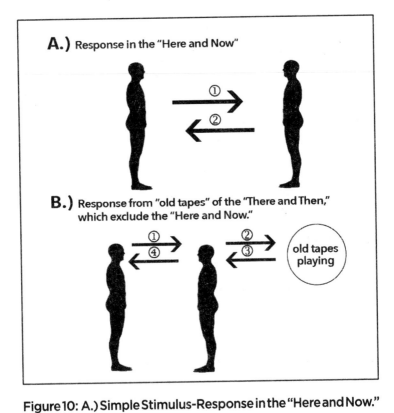

Figure 10: A.) Simple Stimulus-Response in the "Here and Now." B.) Response from the "Old Tapes" of the "There and Then," Which Closes Off Access to the "Here and Now."

Eventually, this belief may become something like *I'm bad when I'm angry*, or *I'm unlovable when I'm angry*. There is typically an unconscious *uh-oh!* sense attached to the end of these Deep False Beliefs. This sense reflects that the survival wiring is involved, and translates to *I'm in danger of losing this very important person who keeps me alive!*

Hypothetically, if a teen or adult came to understand for the first time that they are not supposed to get angry, the effects of this would be minimal. Why? Because this thought is not connected with the fight, flight, or freeze response or complex in the survival brain. Instead, it's just another rule to be mastered without the imminent life and death sense of importance attached to it. Therefore, it is not a Deep False Belief.

An example of this that I used earlier, "It's Wednesday, I need to take out the garbage." This rule is not locked together with a fight, flight, or freeze response complex. Your kitchen might not smell very pleasant if you forget to take out the trash on time, but it is not life-threatening.

Once the fight, flight, or freeze complexes are stored in our brain, they often do not go away. If and when we come to understand that they are not accurate, they still remain locked in place. For example, when I am forty years old and come to finally understand that I don't need to perform well in activities in order to win my parents' love, it makes no difference with the Deep False Belief that is already stored away. I will still become triggered when I don't perform well, even if my prefrontal cortex knows it's silly.

Can you guess why that is?

What part of the brain locked in the fight, flight, or freeze complex during childhood that created the Deep False Belief of, "Whatever I do, I better do well (or else!)? Answer: The unconscious parts of the brain that are related to ancient survival responses and complexes. And what part of the brain came to realize at age forty that this just isn't true? Answer: The conscious prefrontal cortex.

Again, our *understandings* often have little impact on raw survival encoding.

Our conscious thoughts have almost no bearing on the workings of the very powerful and primitive unconscious survival brain areas. The realization that some deeply held but erroneous belief is not true means almost nothing to the survival brain. The Deep False Belief remains and it can still be triggered over and over again. Unless we do something to unlink the powerful primal flight, fight, or freeze complex from the Deep False Belief, we are at its mercy of firing whenever it is triggered! We'll discuss more about this unlinking in the second half of this book.

The next step: While the process of our young brains making up these Deep False Beliefs continues in order to stay safe, our personality is evolving and developing. That's one of the reasons these are called our formative years. Since survival responses trump all other brain wiring, including personality development, we have to develop through and around these many Deep False Beliefs and the landmines of the attached fight, flight, or freeze responses, and a multitude of expectations of ourselves that stem from the Deep False Beliefs. Therefore, the personalities that most of us think of as the very essence of who we are are actually the product of our mind doing its best to create a sense of integrated wholeness—landmines and all! This is all a part of the conditioned, or false self.

Here is a personal example: I always thought I was a naturally tense and high-strung person. That seemed to be part of my personality. But a number of years ago, I found out from relatives, neighbors, and teachers that I was actually a calm, easygoing, and peaceful baby and young child. I learned those stressful behaviors during my early years, both at home, and when academic performance was clearly a major demand and expectation from my parents. The Deep False Belief that my mind created went something like: *I better do well at school, or I will lose Mom and Dad's love. (Uh-oh!)* This belief was tightly bound to a flight/fear response. These were the two components of a "flight—do well or lose love" complex that was stored in my brain. It was always ready and able to trigger me into a feeling of terror about my academic performance.

My parents had often told us as children that my father's job was to work, my mother's job was to take care of the family, and our job as children was to bring home good grades. I was failing miserably at my "job!" For me, most every day was horribly stressful and humiliating. The deeper my brain went into this reaction, the harder it was for me to pay attention in class or do homework. (Remember, this is because the thinking brain goes offline when fight, flight, or freeze responses are running. The thinking brain is the part we mainly use with learning at school.)

I vividly remember sitting on the street curb outside my home, crying, terrified of having to show my parents yet another failed exam that they had to sign off on. This terrible school performance was often followed by parental physical abuse, which only added to my fright. By third grade, I was an anxious kid, and this anxiety and fear had been incorporated into my evolving personality. My more peaceful and quiet nature had become covered up with chronic fear and anxiety.

I ultimately pulled it together for high school and performed very well academically from then on. The high levels of fear and anxiety from so many fight, flight, freeze complexes that had piled up continued. For years, I assumed this high-strung, fearful personality was just who I was.

By the time we are beginning school, most of us have layer upon layer of Deep False Beliefs that are woven together seamlessly within our personalities. We believe this is who we are. We have lost touch with much of our Essential Self. Is it gone, contaminated, or pared down? No—it quietly remains present. But our fight, flight, freeze complexes and Deep False Beliefs are far more attention-grabbing than the quiet whisper of our Essential Self. Therefore, we don't even notice it much of the time. Remember, the Essential Self is a quiet *state of being;* it doesn't manifest through thinking. By its very nature, it's not much of an attention grabber.

Also, remember that fight, flight, or freeze responses are based on the usually unconscious but pervasive fear of dying or being harmed, generated by the ancient survival brain areas.

In contrast, our Essential Self, in its pure form, is based on our inherent nature, e.g., peace, love, happiness, a sense of unity, and a sense of freedom. It is *not* fear- or survival-based. Our creativity and capacity for deep loving relationships and other essential parts of our true nature cannot flourish with too much of the fear-/survival-based programming on board.

Finally, I would like to expand on the personal example I previously shared. In addition to how the personality has to develop through and around our fight, flight, freeze complexes and Deep False Beliefs, an addendum to the story shows an outdated Deep False Belief that is still in action many years later:

I recently took a quiz in a very popular women's magazine that tested a reader's clothing IQ. Even though I have little to no interest in the finesse of clothing and fashion, I took the quiz anyway. As I tallied up my score, I felt my heart drop into the pit of my stomach; my heart was racing, I was breathing rapidly, and my hands actually were trembling. When I realized I had failed the quiz (my score was a big fat zero), I was sickened.

This is an example of how one of my Deep False Beliefs had become deeply embedded in my psyche and was tightly bound to a flight response (fear, anxiety, etc.). This quiz had absolutely no bearing on my adult life. Do I care about the latest and greatest way of tying a scarf? No! Was it important to me to coordinate the color of my nails, shoes, and purse? I think not! Yet, in my unconscious survival brain areas, I did poorly on an exam and this triggered a danger response, all rooted in a childhood Deep False Belief about academic performance.

As you can probably see for yourself, these triggers are time-less and it doesn't matter if you trigger a Deep False Belief one day after it was installed, or thirty years later—it's all the same. The ancient, unconscious survival brain areas have zero concept of time. The perception of time is a creation of the prefrontal cortex. The brain parts that track the passage of time had not yet even begun to evolve when these survival mechanisms were already firmly in place.

When one of these old recordings gets triggered and plays a Deep False Belief tied together with a fight, flight, or freeze response, the actual event of the original incident is not included in the virtual memory. All that is played back is the physical and emotional fight, flight, or freeze experience.

When I did the clothing IQ quiz, my conscious awareness wasn't replaying the childhood horrors of a failed test or yet another disappointing report card. Rather, I was just respond-ing in the current moment to the clothing quiz with anxiety and fright.

This was the *"there and then"* of the past hijacking me out of the *"here and now"* of the present. This translates to the ancient survival brain areas becoming activated. The shift from the here and now to the there and then is *seamlessly* experienced! We are not consciously aware that we have moved from the here and now into a virtual tape playing from the past. Therefore, the past *feels* just as real as the present.

Now, let's go one step further: when we get triggered from an old virtual tape playing, and our body and emotions go back into the fight, flight, or freeze complex it originally held, our thinking brain or prefrontal cortex may notice this shift, and create a rationale for it.

For example, when Jane became depressed when her youngest son, Alex, left for college, her conscious mind created the belief that she became depressed because she now had an empty nest syndrome and her brain chemistry became unbalanced again. She had no conscious awareness that the freeze response that was created when her mother withdrew from her at age two was being retriggered now by another important person leaving her.

When a person has accumulated many of these erroneous, Deep False Beliefs that get triggered, our average daily life has less and less to do with the being-ness state of our Essential Self. Rather, it has more to do with the illusion our brain has created from so many virtual tapes that have come to dominate and co-opt our attention, perceptions, and experience.

A challenging task can be to actually discern what the Deep False Beliefs are! They are so much a part of the background hum of our daily lives that we just don't see many of them. An analogy is the sound of a refrigerator. It runs all the time, but unless we specifically pay attention to it, we usually don't notice it.

Consider this common example. Over the years, I have seen innumerable women in my practice who had childhood experiences of older boys and/or men behaving in a sexually inappropriate manner. As adults, they have a repetitive pattern of not trusting men. A common Deep False Belief that was installed with a fight, flight, or freeze response goes something like: "Men are not safe." The women have no idea that their repetitive experience of men being a danger in their lives may be the old virtual tapes playing. These same tapes play even if the men are safe and mean them no harm. It is manifested in these women by emotional and physical discomfort (from the fight, flight, or freeze response).

Here is an exercise to begin gaining skill at this type of self-reflection. To the best of your ability, try to discern some of the obvious and/or more subtle Deep False Beliefs that run you. I have been practicing this and improving my skill over the years, yet some deeper ones still pop up that I had not seen before. Once you recognize them, you are halfway to letting go of these triggers from your past.

Our minds as children developed most of these beliefs. As we find them, many of them may actually seem silly! Nonetheless, they were once installed and still remain a part of our current "operating system."

Here are some examples of Deep False Beliefs that I have found in my own psyche. Before you make your own list, also take another look at the list on page 102.

Life should be fair!

Whatever I do, I must do well!
    (To review, how do I know this is a deep false belief versus any garden-variety belief? Because I would become anxious whenever I wouldn't do well. That

means it is attached to a fight/flight/freeze response.
Regular beliefs are not.)

I must fit in.

(Again, how do I know it's a deep false belief?
Because I have a fight/flight/freeze response when I
don't fit in. In my case, I become angry, which is a fight
response.)

I don't have as much value as my brother.

I'm defective. There's something wrong with me.

Girls are not as valuable as boys.

I'm not lovable.

Others know better what is right for me.

Most people, especially women, *settle* and shortchange themselves in order to avoid triggering so many of their fight, flight,
freeze complexes.

Write down a few of your Deep False Beliefs, followed by how you know that's what they are versus regular beliefs:

_____

_____

_____

_____

_____

_____

_____

_____

Key Points

1. Children's minds create Deep False Beliefs to both maintain their connection with their caregivers and to minimize the chance of primitive fight, flight, or freeze responses from firing. These are jarring and highly uncomfortable experiences for all people, but especially children, as they are not yet equipped to buffer or prevent them.

2. Deep False Beliefs are often hard to identify in ourselves because they can be hidden in the background hum of our lives. Most of them have been with us since we were children and they often are seamlessly blended with our most basic sense of ourselves. Once we recognize them, they become increasingly easy to find. They lose much of their power over us upon being recognized. They can also get "cleaned out" with certain interventions that we will cover later.

3. These Deep False Beliefs are strongly correlated with the people who were most important to our survival during childhood. When we were young children, our ancient survival brain areas (the brainstem and limbic brain) perceived our caregivers as the most important people for our survival. Most of these Deep False Beliefs created during these early years of life are all about keeping our connections with them. When we are school age, our ancient

survival brain areas perceive our peer group as most
important for survival. Therefore, our brain thinks we are
most vulnerable to endangerment if we stand out from
the peer group.

4. The ancient survival areas of the brain have zero compre-
    hension or understanding of our reality, which is irrelevant
    to the functioning of our ancient survival brain areas. Simi-
    larly, accuracy is also irrelevant to these brain areas.

5. Fight, flight or freeze complexes are created when a poten-
    tial fight, flight, or freeze response becomes bound together
    with some type of perception, experience, person, etc. Deep
    False Beliefs develop from a fight, flight, or freeze response
    becoming bound together with a belief. This means that if a
    Deep False Belief is triggered, a fight, flight, or freeze com-
    plex response will automatically fire. This complex is stored
    in the brain and can go on to fire or be triggered for many
    years—long after the belief has any relevance in our lives.

6. During our formative years, from birth until roughly age
    twenty, our personalities have to develop through and
    around these many Deep False Beliefs, and the land mines
    of the related fight, flight, freeze responses. Therefore,
    many aspects of our personalities are based on the Deep
    False Beliefs and conditioning we experienced while
    growing up.

7. Throughout all of this intense adjusting of our child mind to these overpowering ancient survival brain area activities, our Essential Self remains in its ever quiet state of being. But our attention is now far, far away. By the end of childhood, most of us have long forgotten who and/or what we really are. As a result, we suffer.

Principles of Essential Living

- *To the degree we consciously connect with our Essential Self, we have peace, happiness, a sense of freedom, and a feeling of unity, love, and truth.*

- *To the degree we are not connected with our Essential Self, we suffer.*

- *We don't notice our true self—our very essence—even though it is right in front of us, because our mind is too intense to notice the quiet and still Essential Self.*

Chapter 6

Expectations, Negative Feelings, and Symptoms

L et's move to the next step: expectations generated by our Deep False Beliefs.

Expectations

Crystal is a twenty-one-year-old college student in the midst of her junior year. She recently moved to off-campus housing with some friends, because she was tiring of dorm life and wanted to get a taste of living more independently. Within the next few weeks, she has to declare a major, and become more focused on her studies and preparing for a career. Some of her friends have recently become engaged or married, or are in serious romantic relationships, which has made Crystal more aware that she also needs to begin expanding her horizons in this department. Her anxiety levels began increasing as she felt unable to meet these expectations of herself. They finally reached a level that was affecting her sleep, academic performance, and other areas of her life, so she entered into psychotherapy.

Being on the cusp of adulthood may be a very welcome time for many people but less so for others. Many of the large and encompassing life expectations for our early adulthood have been planted in our minds years earlier. Is there anything wrong with Crystal's newly surfacing expectations of herself? Not on the surface; however, she is entering the phase of life where many people take giant steps *away* from their awareness of the Essential Self. As we begin to fully assume the responsibilities of adulthood, most of us more firmly push aside our Essential Self.

In Crystal's case, the relevant Deep False Beliefs, with their resulting "expectations" were far too stringent and suffocating. For example, one of her Deep False Beliefs is, "Whatever I do, I better do *perfectly.*" Both of her parents were perfectionists and her mind created very strict Deep False Beliefs with overly demanding expectations. Once she recognized this, she quickly toned it down and felt great relief.

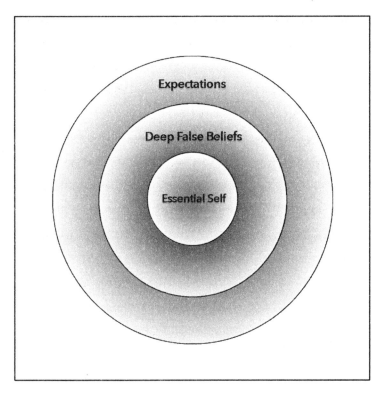

Figure 11: The Addition of Expectations.

As we grow up from childhood through young adulthood and then full-blown adulthood, our multitude of Deep False Beliefs need to somehow be connected to how we actually live our lives. One of the ways our mind accomplishes this is through creating expectations of ourselves and others. These are what enable us to translate our Deep False Beliefs into how we carry out our daily lives. Think for a minute about that. If one of your Deep False Beliefs from early childhood is *Whatever I do, I better do well,* how do you actually make that happen? We form an enormous number of self-expectations from even just this one of Deep False Belief. For example, the expectation of good grades at school or excellent performance in athletics may become offshoots of the Deep False Belief of *Whatever I do, I better do well.* How many expectations could spin off from this one belief? I would guesstimate many thousands! A few categories are expectations of what makes me a good person, successful, how I should relate to others, etc.

As I mentioned earlier, I once spent an entire day writing down all of my thoughts. I was amazed to find that I had expectations to do well with many things. For example, how well did I brush my teeth; did I do my hair nicely; did I eat right for breakfast; did I drive too fast or too slow to work; was I nice enough to others, etc. Even though this one Deep False Belief was installed in many of us when we were children, our brain still adds to the list of further expectations. Remember, we each have many thousands of these Deep False Beliefs. So how many expectations are we walking around with? If we do the math, I think we're looking at a vast amount of expectations that are stored within our brain. It could easily be hundreds of thousands or possibly in the million range. And, by the way, when you have expectations of yourself, do you think you also have similar expectations of others? You bet!

Over the years, Deep False Beliefs and their offshoot expectations develop into layers, much like those of an onion. This is why many children, if receiving interventions that address these ancient survival brain areas, can heal much more quickly than adults because they don't have layer upon layer of "baggage" that we adults have.

Once again, what is happening with our Essential Self as our mind/brain becomes inundated with expectations? Our attention turns further and further away. Is our Essential Self changing in any way, or leaving, or becoming contaminated? No. It just quietly and peacefully awaits our return. Since it is timeless, the Essential Self is not in any rush.

As we move from the Essential Self → Deep False Beliefs → Expectations, we become more and more symptomatic. *The more we turn our attention away from our Essential Self, the more symptomatic we become.* The symptoms could be depression, sadness, anxiety, ulcers, feelings of emptiness, confusion, backaches, etc. The more we disconnect from our Essential Self, and become increasingly symptomatic, our risk for self-medicating gets higher and higher. This self-medicating could take place with alcohol, drugs, food, sex, shopping, the internet, television, busy-ness, gambling, intensity with exercise, sports, and many others.

I often tell patients and audiences I address to think of our Essential Self as analogous to the direction of north on a compass. The farther the compass needle points away from our Essential Self, which means our lives are not aligned with our Essential Self, the more we suffer.

Now It's Your Turn . . .

Let's move from theory and into the reality of your life. To the best of your ability, see if you can identify a Deep False Belief that has had a grip on your life. You can pick one from your list at the end of the last chapter, or identify another one now.

Write the Deep False Belief in one sentence:

_____

_____

_____

What are some of the expectations that flow from that one Deep False Belief? Try to stretch yourself to identify as many as possible. Reflect broadly on your life to answer this question.

a) _____

_____

_____

b) _____

_____

_____

c) _____

_____

_____

d) _____

_____

_____

e) _____

_____

_____

f) _____

_____

_____

g) _____

_____

_____

Please continue on a separate piece of paper, if needed.

Even when you are done with this exercise, keep noticing and jotting down other expectations you see that flow from this one belief. This is great practice for the self-reflection skill that is so valuable for ultimately reconnecting with your Essential Self.

Negative Feelings and Symptoms

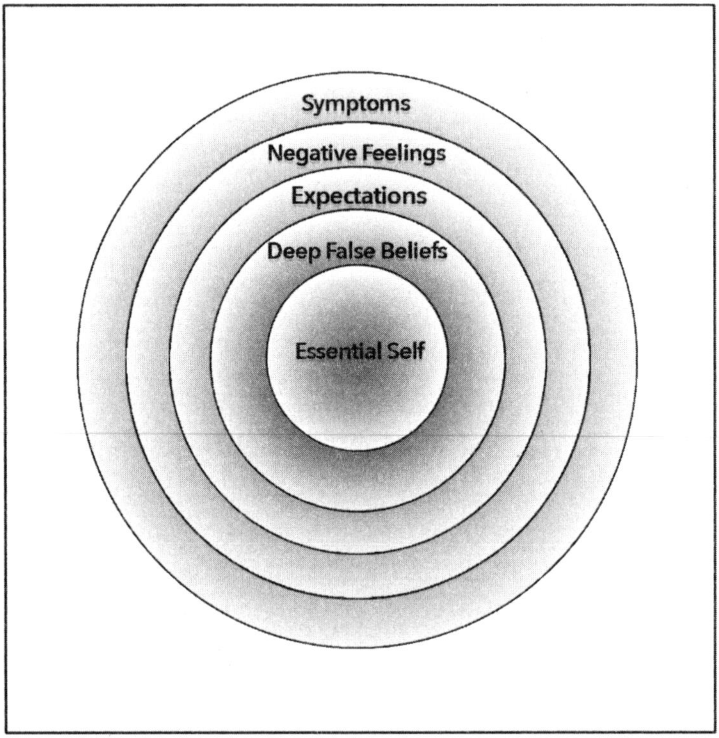

**Figure 12: The Addition of Negative Feelings
and Symptoms**

As our lives proceed, many of us find we are not succeeding in some of our expectations that had been put into place many years earlier. With the common Deep False Belief that we have to do everything well, we find that we simply cannot do as many things as well as we used to. For example, we may find that we cannot perform as well in sports anymore, or that our marriages didn't work out as we had expected, or that our health isn't as robust as it used to be, etc.

People who were raised with Deep False Beliefs that were really severe, generally discover much earlier in their lives that they aren't meeting their expectations. For example, the people I've met or worked with who had a Deep False Belief that went something like *Whatever I do, I better do perfectly!* Like Crystal, they typically begin to have significant failures with their expectations earlier than most others. Why? Because humans are not capable of being perfect, or doing things perfectly on a regular basis. These people tend to experience tremendous inner stress, expecting themselves to live their lives in accordance with the impossible.

Russ is a fifty-eight-year-old CEO of a multi-facility health-care company. He was a remarkably successful young man who grew a single, small health-care facility into a corporation that owns twenty-three hospitals. Here is one of his Deep False Beliefs: "The degree of success that I have in my career, is the degree to which I am an important and valuable person." (Of course, the Deep False Belief that runs a little deeper than this goes something like, "I am only valued to the degree I succeed." A little deeper than that may be, "I am not inherently worthy.") The expectations that were offshoots of this Deep False Belief included, "I will do whatever it takes to be successful" and "When the going gets tough, the tough get going."

He began faltering at meeting his expectations when he developed a chronic medical illness that left him far too weak to go any further with his business plans or even maintain the ones he had already developed. As a result, Russ became severely depressed. It was only when he sought help for the depression that he began to see how his erroneous beliefs from childhood and his driven and intense expectations had ultimately led to his current state of depression. This case had a very happy ending. As Russ began discovering his Essential Self and found great joy and peace, his health significantly improved and he was able to engage in his work again. Except this time, his work had greater personal meaning for him as his Deep False Beliefs were no longer driving his expectations for great success.

If we look at the diagram on page 128, we see that negative feelings may follow when our expectations are not met. Specifically, these negative feelings include anger, fear, or sadness. Research has clearly shown that when we harbor negative feelings for longer than very brief periods of time, our bodies can become negatively impacted; for example, our immune function, heart function, resistance to cancer, heart disease, cognitive function, etc., may become compromised. From this, we end up in the outermost circle of the diagram, which is when we develop symptoms. These could be the symptoms listed above and/or many others.[5, 6]

Depending upon the makeup of each of our inborn tendencies, psychological makeup, genetics, epigenetics (that is, related to the turning on/off of genes), health vulnerabilities, etc., this determines who is predisposed to what. For example, when my sister experiences these negative emotions for more than a brief period of time, her stomach begins to act up. I've not had her problems, but I do become overly anxious. Other people become depressed, get headaches, backaches, physical issues, or addictions. Over the years, these symptoms can become compounded and create even more psychological and medical problems.

The final outer circle of the diagram depicts the last step in our sliding down the black hole away from our Essential Self. We humans usually wait until we are plagued by the symptoms level of the diagram before we do anything about it. But that's okay, whatever it takes. This is the hidden value of symptoms and suffering: they frequently motivate us to take action!

By the time we are adults, most of us have brains and nervous systems that are inundated with Deep False Beliefs, expectations, fight, flight, freeze responses, chronic negative feelings, and symptoms. We've typically long forgotten our Essential Self. Our compass needle is pointing far away from north. It would be challenging to follow Shakespeare's admonition in *Hamlet,* "To thine own self be true," simply because most of us are unaware of who the self even is!

This is the hidden value of symptoms and suffering: they frequently motivate us to take action!

Trying to Find Our Way Back

Even though our attention has long ago turned away from our Essential Self, we are powerfully, but unconsciously, trying to return to it.

Even though our attention has long ago turned away from our Essential Self, we are powerfully, but unconsciously, trying to return to it. We seek success in the ways we were raised and conditioned to view success, or the way our mind views success. But deep down, we think that we will acquire the inherent qualities of our Essential Self when we attain these worldly successes. This is what the exercises in Chapter 1 were about—what you identified at the surface of your life that you want most, followed by digging deeper to find that you are really seeking the qualities of your Essential Self. In our culture, success is rarely equated with turning our attention back to our Essential Self. But attaining success in work, finances, relationships, or other typical realms does not directly reconnect us with our Essential Self.

In our culture, success is rarely equated with turning our attention back to our Essential Self.

List three ways you've tried to reconnect with the real you—or your Essential Self—through work, finances, relationships, or any other way.

1. _____

_____

_____

2. _____

_____

_____

3. _____

_____

_____

List three symptoms that you believe may be related to your having turned away from your Essential Self.

1. _____

_____

_____

2. _____

_____

_____

3. _____

_____

_____

Now, list three of the ways you may self-medicate your stress from having turned away from your Essential Self.

1. _____

_____

_____

2. _____

_____

_____

3. _____

_____

_____

Key Points

1. From Deep False Beliefs naturally flow expectations. These are what enable us to integrate our Deep False Beliefs in our lives.

2. Most of us have hundreds of thousands of expectations of ourselves and others. By the time we are young adults, most of our thoughts and behaviors are the products of our childhood Deep False Beliefs and their expectations. This process quietly infiltrates and gradually "squeezes out" the space for the experience and expression of our Essential Self.

3. We become symptomatic with emotional, physical, and spiritual problems that arise from our turning away from our Essential Self. The degree to which we have turned away from our Essential Self is the degree to which we suffer.

4. We resort to self-medicating the discomfort and suffering, and may develop addictions. The self-medicating can be substances, like alcohol, drugs, or food; activities, like sex, gambling, shopping, overworking, staying too busy, fantasizing, surfing the internet, and watching too much television; and "intensity junkie" behaviors, such as extreme sports, driving too fast, and generally taking unnecessary risks for the rush of adrenaline.

5. We then have the problem of being disconnected from our Essential Self *and* the problems from self-medicating.

6. Deep down, we think that we will acquire the inherent qualities of our Essential Self when we attain worldly successes. But this rarely works. However, people who seek and reconnect with the Essential Self often derive greater enjoyment from their worldly successes.

Principles of Essential Living

- *Symptoms (i.e., suffering) can be a good thing! Symptoms make us uncomfortable and motivate us to do something, to change.*

- *Ultimately, we all want the same thing: to reconnect with our Essential Self (our true and inherent nature).*

- *As children, we lose conscious connection with our Essential Self. We forget who we are. We begin to suffer. This is the product of evolutionary brain glitch.*

- *As children, we become captivated by our outside world. It is far more emotionally charged, both positively and negatively, than our still Essential Self. Our mind loves this greater excitement and drama!*

- *Attaining success in work, finances, relationships, etc., cannot substitute for reconnecting with our Essential Self.*

- *To the degree we are not connected with our Essential Self, we suffer.*

Part 2:

The Way Home

Chapter 7

The Big Game Plan for Reconnecting with Our Essential Self

U ltimately, what would be the most effective and efficient strategy for healing from this whole process? Let's begin Part 2 to take a look.

At this point, we have fallen all the way down the rabbit hole—from our Essential Self to our Deep False Beliefs; to our expectations of self and others; to our negative feelings; and finally to symptoms and/or addictions. If you are like most people, you have long forgotten your Essential Self.

Before we explore any further, let's look at some general guidelines, a few of which have been mentioned earlier, to help you on your journey.

1. *Reclaiming our Essential Self is our birthright!*

   In my opinion, this is the most important thing a person can do in their lifetime. Most people only reach this conclusion when they are facing death. Why wait?

   I have also spoken with many parents who described feeling selfish if they seek their Essential Self, as they believe their children should be their top priority. My opinion is that is the very best thing a parent can model for a child or teenager is this process. In effect, you would be saying to them through word and deed that it is wonderful to seek to know who you are. Kids are usually very happy to have their parents do this, and it gives them permission to follow suit.

   Can you think of a more generous gift to a child than giving them their Essential Self back?

2. *Reexamine the life goals of comfort and taking it easy.*

   There is a common fallacy in our culture regarding striving for comfort and taking it easy as our primary life goals. There is an unspoken assumption that we should ultimately seek comfort and enjoyment. Many people spend the majority of their adult years with this as their ultimate goal. Take a closer look and see if it is really true for you. The vast majority of people I have known who dig a little deeper, find that these two items can be very nice to have, but they are not what is most important in their lives. The people who do want these seem to want them more as a doorway to connecting with aspects of their Essential Self. For example: "Yes, I wished I had taken it easier in my life so that I could have had more time with my spouse and enjoyed my kids more." This is the pursuit of love, one of the inherent qualities of our Essential Self.

3. *Continue to identify what is most important to you.*

   I cannot overestimate this! Your understanding of what is most important to you is usually an ongoing process. If you keep at it, what's most important to you will reveal itself more clearly and deeply over time. With each and every step, welcome the deeper awareness and understandings that surface. Doing such a compass check at least a few times each year may be very helpful in staying on your course!

4. *Honor what you find.*

   As you become increasingly aware of what is most important to you, honor it! This is *so* important! There is a huge difference between understanding something and living your life aligned with that understanding. As I became more and more aware of how important truth is in my life, I would welcome the awareness of truth as it arose in many different situations, and would act on it accordingly.

   For example, several years ago, I was talking with a hospital administrator who was getting on my nerves. I suddenly became aware she was ultimately the same "perfectly imperfect" person as I was, and had the exact same inherent worth that I had. I welcomed this understanding and felt warmth and caring toward her, and related to her accordingly. This is an example of how to honor whatever is most important to you and arises in you.

Note that my shift in attitude and opening of my heart did not come from a feeling of "should" nor an ideal. Rather it was from the recognition of the truth of her humanity and mine. What I used to do was focus on my thoughts of how immature she was and noticed all of her other flaws, as if I didn't have them!

Most people who get these epiphanies of truth are very moved by them, but then go on with their lives without applying what they had just seen or come to understand. Pretty soon, these truths are forgotten.

5. *Patience*

Although we all have this very clean and clear Essential Self, we also have ancient survival areas in our brains that are still alive and well. Our newer brain areas are retrofitted on top of the old. Our human mind is loaded with flaws and glitches! As a matter of fact, most of this book is about cutting our way through the jungle

Most of this book is about cutting our way through the jungle of out-of-date and old version survival software and wiring that is obsolete for our species. Just see yourself and others as "works in progress."

of out-of-date and old version survival software and wiring that is obsolete for our species. Just see yourself and others as "works in progress." Remember, our Essential Self doesn't change or evolve, but our

> Remember, our Essential Self doesn't change or evolve, but our mind's ability to recognize our Essential Self, and get out of the way, can always use more refinement.

mind's ability to recognize our Essential Self, and get out of the way, can always use more refinement.

6. *Practice good self-care.*

I will be elaborating on this throughout the rest of this book. Good self-care is important for us wherever we are in our life. Our life's journey can be so much better supported when we are practicing good self-care. I used to think that the term "good self-care" was hogwash; similar to parental directions, such as "Brush your teeth, eat your vegetables, go to sleep early, *blah, blah, blah . . .*" But over the past several years, I came to realize how important it actually is. Stephen Covey, in his timeless classic *The Seven Habits of Highly Effective People*[7] talks about the importance of "sharpening the saw." It means "preserving and enhancing the greatest asset you have—you. It means having a balanced program for self-renewal. Without this discipline, the body becomes weak, the mind mechanical, the emotions raw, the spirit insensitive, and the person selfish."

I think of good self-care as very similar to sharpening the saw. No matter what else we are working on in our lives, practicing good self-care is really important. *It supports us to consistently be present in our lives.* For example, if you are one of the many folks who walk around sleep-deprived, it is more difficult to be aware of and connect with your Essential Self.

7. *Whatever we place our time and attention on dictates what unfolds in our lives.*

   For most people, it's not until we are in a life-threatening situation or near death that we come to see the difference between the false self and the Essential Self. In the big picture, wouldn't it be wise to do what it takes to shift more of our attention and time to our Essential Self? Our lives will unfold in the direction of where we place our time and attention.

> *Our lives will unfold in the direction of where we place our time and attention.*

Now let's look at how can we optimize a plan for reclaiming our Essential Self. Here are three potential general strategies.

1. We can decrease the excess amount of fight, flight, and freeze complexes that are held and stuck in our nervous system. I refer to this as "Calling off the Dogs."
2. We can strengthen certain brain areas that support our reconnecting with the Essential Self.
3. We can place our attention on our Essential Self, and increasingly align our lives with it.

Do we have to do the first two before the third? No! The purpose of the first two is to help us open doors to the third, to whatever degree we can tune into our Essential Self, and align our lives with it, with or without the first two items. Do we have to go in order of the three things? No, not necessarily. Many people can start right away with practices that support the second or third item. Similarly, many people engage in practices that involve all three aspects of the plan. Getting professional guidance before embarking on a plan is highly recommended.

The Big Game Plan

It is important to have a plan of action for important events, and what could be more important than living your life to the fullest? With that in mind, let's move on to a potential "Game Plan" for reclaiming your Essential Self.

From here on, we will look at potential avenues for actively reorganizing the game plan of our lives. Many of us have been running on autopilot for most of our adult years, just like our parents and grandparents did. But to reach the upper levels of Maslow's Hierarchy of Needs, you just can't run on autopilot. When we do, it is usually from our survival-based false self. There are exceptions to this, but don't depend on it.

The game plan I am presenting here is just an idea for a starting point to inspire you. Feel free to use any or none of it. As you become more focused on your own path, your Essential

Self may naturally guide you in a direction that feels the most right for you.

For example, there have been a few times in my life where I had a certain game plan for reconnecting with the Essential Self, and had been very successful. But after gaining some real clarity, I became aware of how I needed to shift gears. My revised game plan changed accordingly and turned out to be accurate for me. The important thing for now is to just get started! As the athletic shoe ads used to say so succinctly, "Just Do It!"

The greatest step of all for most people is the simple decision to turn the spotlight of their attention inward, instead of always pointing it outward.

> *The greatest step of all for most people is the simple decision to turn the spotlight of their attention inward, instead of always pointing it outward.*

Before We Do Anything . . .

Before we can comfortably shift the spotlight of our attention from an almost exclusively outer world—people, jobs, money, and family—to include our inner state of being, most people need to have adequate emotional and mental stability.

Before some people can comfortably and safely embark on a path inward, they may need to address any severe existing addiction and/or mental health problems that can short-circuit their efforts to turn inward.

Clues that someone may need to get better stabilized are any extremes in symptoms or severe diagnoses. For example, severe

depression, severe anxiety, panic attacks, any psychosis, halluci-
nations, delusions, active mania and hypomania, suicidal and/
or homicidal thoughts/plans, tendency toward violence, severe
eating disorder, serious addictions, including severe degrees
of gambling, sex addiction, chemical dependency, and many
others. These are examples of some of the symptoms and diagnoses that are serious enough that they may interfere with someone
trying to do this inner work. Even if someone has the very best
of intentions, they may still need to first get stabilized.

For people who may have any significant symptoms or
diagnoses, or are not sure if they do, it is wisest to first get the
approval of a licensed and certified mental health professional
before embarking on this inner path.

Similarly, if someone is taking medications prescribed or recommended by a health care professional, it may be unwise and
potentially dangerous to change or stop without first checking
with the health care provider.

People who are engaged in any serious addictive behaviors
may need to become clean, sober, and/or abstinent for a while
before proceeding. Again, it is wise to first consult with an expert
in the addictions field.

When we are experiencing these symptoms/disorders ourselves, it is often difficult to be objective about the severity of our
problems. This is one of the reasons it is wise to first get approval
from a mental health professional before proceeding; they won't
have the same "blind spots."

After Stabilizing . . .

For people who may have some of the above mentioned problems but have now stabilized, and for people who are pretty well balanced and don't have severe addictive and/or severe mental health symptoms or diagnoses, I have found what follows in the pages ahead invaluable.

Chapter 8

Adopting an Inner Framework

For many people, adopting an inner framework may be all you need. Over the years, I have noticed that the people who have an underlying framework or model from which they orient and align their lives each and every day tend to get better results reconnecting with the Essential Self. Many don't need to utilize the interventions and techniques in the chapters that follow, although they might choose to for additional benefit.

The five frameworks that I am presenting here are the ones with which I am most familiar. There are many other frameworks and models I am simply not addressing, as I am not as familiar with them.

I am often asked if people can count their religious traditions as a framework or model. Very often, yes! The bottom line to be looking for, with whatever framework you use, is if there is progress in your reconnecting with the Essential Self.

What should be common to all frameworks? They should be capable of being used any time, any place, and in almost any situation. They should offer ways to be utilized when we become "stuck" in any interactions that don't feel right, and more generally inform us how to proceed in a manner that is better aligned with our Essential Self.

If someone's religious tradition or other frameworks/models do not offer all of the aforementioned, there may be no problem with integrating it with another framework. For example, the twelve-step model strongly recommends that people's religious traditions become a daily, integral part of practicing the Twelve Steps.

If any of the five frameworks that I describe here appeal to you, get additional information from the internet, books, CDs, websites, meetings, etc.

I will present these five now, followed by a description of the path I took with three of them. I will go into greater detail with the first framework, as it is potentially an invaluable tool for reconnecting with the Essential Self.

First Framework:
Overview of Developmental Immaturity

Pia Mellody developed her "Overview of Developmental Immaturity"—also known as The Meadows Model or Pia Mellody's Model—in the 1980's. She went on to publish four books that were related to it. The three that are most relevant to this subject are *Facing Codependence*, the accompanying workbook *Breaking Free*, and *The Intimacy Factor*. She has also available many CDs and DVDs, and offers workshops.[8, 9, 10, 11] Her website is *www.PiaMellody.com*.

I have been using her framework for many years with great success. Not only do I utilize it for understanding each of my clients' areas of "stuckness," but also as my own personal roadmap for remaining connected with the Essential Self.

This model contains five Core Issues to which most people can easily relate. When a person optimizes their functioning in any of these areas, they become able to reconnect with their Essential Self. The more of these Core Issues that a person comes into greater balance with, the greater their access to the Essential Self.

While practicing this model over time, and concurrently engaging in some of the items described in the upcoming chapter on "Calling Off the Dogs" and other chapters, I have consistently seen people have great success in reconnecting with their Essential Self.

This model can be utilized even when our lives are going great and we're feeling good. I find myself still optimizing the five core issues, as it helps me find and let go of more of the false self, which leaves the Essential Self increasingly self-evident.

Let's take a closer look at the five Core Issues of Pia Mellody's model.

1. The First Core Issue: "Self Esteem"

The important point here is identifying *how* you esteem yourself. (Notice that I used the word *"esteem"* as a verb.) To the degree that you esteem yourself from what others think of you, or how favorably you compare your value and worth to others, is the degree to which your self-esteem can fluctuate, sometimes wildly. This leads to suffering. It is similar to a roller-coaster ride. Your self-esteem can be high for a period of time, low at others, and anything in between. This can sap much of your attention and energy. Esteeming yourself from others does not match the reality of your having inherent value and worth.

Esteeming yourself from others does not match the reality of your having inherent value and worth.

The truth is we all have inherent value and worth. When we behave less than ideally, our inherent worth, which is a part of our Essential Self, does not change at all. Similarly, when we behave really well, or have great success, our value and worth do not increase even one iota. Everyone is different from everyone else, but we all have the same inherent worth. We can't add to it, or lessen it, no matter what we do or don't do.

Therefore, the degree to which we esteem ourselves from our *inherent worth*, rather than from others or our own judgments, leaves us with far greater stability and compassion for ourselves and others. When we primarily esteem ourselves from the value that is inherently a part of our Essential Self, it doesn't increase when we do well at something, nor decrease when we do poorly. It is stable because it has nothing to do with performance of any kind. When we feel increasingly at peace with this, we automatically can see the same thing in others. Relationships begin to feel so much richer and more stable!

Our culture, most families, workplaces, and educational systems are extremely biased toward teaching us to esteem ourselves from what others think of us, how well we perform at school, sports, etc., and/or how we think we compare to others. This leaves us at the mercy of our constantly shifting judgments about ourselves and others; always trying to feel good about ourselves. *Practicing esteeming ourselves from our inherent worth is usually the only way to break the old habits of esteeming ourselves from outside of our inherent worth.* However, many of the practices, readings, techniques, and therapies that are described throughout the rest of the book can facilitate the ease with which we can make this transition that takes us closer to the truth of who we are.

> *Practicing esteeming ourselves from our inherent worth is usually the only way to break the old habits of esteeming ourselves from outside of our inherent worth.*

When we comfortably reside within our own skin, feeling worthy by virtue of the fact that we have inherent worth, we are reconnecting with our Essential Self.

2. The Second Core Issue: "Boundaries"

As newborns, we don't come pre-packaged with boundaries. Have you ever heard a newborn say to its caregivers, "Hey! Back off here! You're not giving me enough space!" We are born 100 percent vulnerable and we depend upon our caregivers to relate to us with appropriate boundaries and to ultimately teach us about practicing good boundaries later in childhood. Children's nervous systems become stressed and possibly traumatized when caregivers are either too emotionally distant or, at the other extreme, "smothering" a child.

On our path of reconnection with our Essential Self, it is really important that we exercise our ability to say "no" to that which is not true for us, and then actively exclude it. Conversely, we can say "yes" to that which is true for us and allow it into our life. People who have been raised with caregivers that are smothering or too distant often have difficulty setting and enforcing the boundaries in their lives that enable them to exclude or incorporate whatever they need.

For example, Ralph was raised in a family where both parents were emotionally smothering in many ways. Almost all decisions were made for Ralph, even many years after he was old enough to make his own choices, For example, which clothes to buy, who to spend time with, playing the family's favorite sports. The unconscious pattern that developed for him was a strong tendency to avoid analyzing what was and wasn't true for him. This was followed by an inability to exercise his power in letting go of people, situations, and choices that were not true or right for him, or inviting people into his life who felt right to him. Although this is a more extreme example, it applies to the exceedingly common situation of parents raising kids without conscious awareness of good boundaries.

As an adult, Ralph now has difficulty reflecting upon that which is true for him or not true for him, and then acting accordingly. For example, he wavers about who to date, what type of work he would like to do, and more basically, what he thinks or feels about various people, politics, etc. Due to being smothered for so long, *Ralph lost touch with his own reality and took on his parents' reality as his own.*

In a related vein, a big part of reclaiming our Essential Self is identifying who/what we are *not* and integrating this awareness into our lives. There is no substitute for the power of discernment that is derived from practicing good physical and emotional boundaries. This is an essential skill needed for reclaiming our Essential Self, and remaining connected with it.

3. The Third Core Issue: "Reality"

This is one of the most important Core Issues. It is where the rubber meets the road!

When we are born, we are fully in touch with our reality, although we lack any conscious awareness of it. When we are babies and toddlers, we can't exist or express anything but our own reality! But by the time many of us reach approximately age two, emotional areas of our brain are becoming more active and there is a new level of intensity in what we feel and how we behave. Many children experience the increased limit setting and reprimanding from their caregivers as personally shaming and attacking, even if caregivers are just addressing the *behavior* of the child, and not the child him/herself.

During this early life stage, a majority of children step out of their own reality. The ancient survival brain areas of young children believe that the most important thing the child can do is to keep the love and approval of their caregivers. When the child perceives—accurately or inaccurately—that the caregiver is attacking or shaming their reality, they begin to abandon it. They consciously move more into being a "good" child so as not to threaten their relationship with the caregiver.

As practical as this may seem for a child who wants to maintain and thrive in their connection with their caregiver, *this is a huge step toward the child turning away from their Essential Self.*

Why? Because as adults, most of us have long forgotten how we genuinely feel or experience many things. We stepped out of our own reality at such a young age that many of us forgot it was even there. Now, as adults, as we try to find our way back home, we don't know where that "thread" is, so that we can pick it up again and follow it back to our own reality.

We usually must be in touch with our own reality to reconnect with the Essential Self. Therefore, reconnecting with our reality at any given point in time is an extremely important practice because it is never too late to find our way back.

Family traditions and expectations often influence and worsen this process. For example, in my childhood home, playing tennis was considered of great importance and was highly valued. As soon as I could walk and hold a racket at the same time without tipping over, I was playing tennis. Weather permitting, our family members engaged in this activity together nearly every day. After I left home, I played on my college tennis team for a while. I just *loved* tennis—or did I?

When I was in my late twenties and engaged in my own psychotherapy as a part of my training as a psychiatrist, it suddenly dawned on me that I actually *didn't* like tennis. I actually hated it and haven't touched a racket ever since!

How could I have missed this for so many years? Because I had deeply ignored so many things in my own reality throughout my early life. Tennis was one way to maintain my connection with my parents. However, tennis was one of the many items out of tune with my own truth. When I was growing up, not playing tennis was not even a consideration. My parents loved tennis, therefore I loved tennis. They never considered that I might not share their passion.

As a child, I didn't have much choice in the matter so I learned another game—that of ignoring my own reality and conforming to someone else's. All these years later, I understand the

Ignoring our own reality in favor of conforming to someone else's is a major impediment in the work to reclaim our Essential Self!

importance of *not* doing this. Knowing our own reality is the most basic skill for being able to identify what is true for each of us—and, conversely, what is not true. Ignoring our own reality in favor of conforming to someone else's is a major impediment in the work to reclaim our Essential Self!

4. The Fourth Core Issue: "Dependency"

Placing a priority on practicing good self-care is the essential premise of this core issue.

For various reasons, many people are raised to pay more attention to, and place more value upon, others' emotional or physical needs rather than their own. While generosity and altruism are good qualities, placing others' needs ahead of our own as a matter of course is something altogether different. The often hidden value judgment within these families is that we are better people if we take care of others first, more so than practicing good self-care. For example, many children grow up in families where their role as a "good" child includes helping their mother or father feel better when they are down, or using the child as a sounding board for their problems. This is often not in the best interests of the parents or the children.

Children need to learn from adults how to take care of their own needs. When caregivers don't adequately teach them how to practice good self-care, the child may not fully grasp the concept.

This often leads to children growing into adults that just don't know their own needs or wants, and therefore, how to take care of themselves.

Likewise, this is another roadblock on the path to reconnecting with our Essential Self. If we have been conditioned to ignore our own wants and needs, we don't notice an inner calling to know our Essential Self.

Similarly, if a child is shamed or attacked for having wants and needs, they will quickly bury them and forget they even exist. The interest in our Essential Self often goes out the window with everything else.

5. The Fifth Core Issue: "Moderation"

In order to find the necessary balance to go after something that we want, we have to be in touch with the power of our inborn spontaneity, yet rein it in enough that it is not too intense and destructive to ourselves or others. On one end of the spectrum, we may possess so much intensity that it turns others off to us. Conversely, when we have too little access to our inborn spontaneity, we may go through life shut down and unable to actualize that which is important to us. This is why moderation of spontaneity is so important to our success in seeking our Essential Self.

As we gradually come to center in one or more of these five core issues, our Essential Self becomes increasingly evident.

Quieting the excessive fight, flight, and freeze in our bodies and nervous system, and/or strengthening certain other brain areas, enable us to come to center in these five core issues much more quickly. This is true for all five of these frameworks/models. All of them enable us to derive better results from each of the items in the following chapters, and vice versa. They synergize with each other.

Second Framework: "The Work" by Byron Katie

"The Work" was developed by Byron Katie in the mid-1980's. She has written many books, but *Loving What Is*[12] is a really excellent place to learn to utilize her four-step "inquiry" practice. She also has produced many CDs, DVDs, has free phone-in assistance, online videos, workshops, webinars, and podcasts. Much of her online material is free.

"The Work" consists of a short series of questions and "Turnarounds" that you ask yourself when you find yourself figuratively bumping into people, situations, relationships, and feelings that bother you, or just don't feel quite right. Most things we find or experience as stressful, actually are reflections of thoughts that are not true. For example, I may feel stressed and bothered when people are rude to me. My stress is coming from my underlying thought and belief that people should not be rude to others. But in a deep sense, is that true? If I let myself quietly sit with this question, and allow a deeper truth to bubble up into my conscious mind, I find that my thought is not necessarily true. In most situations, people's rude behavior is *their* business. The fact that I have a belief that "X" shouldn't happen creates my own suffering.

Byron Katie says, "There are three types of business in this world: my business, your business, and God's business. When I get into your business or God's business, I suffer; but only every time." So, when someone is rude to me that is their business. As long as I hold onto the belief that they shouldn't do that; I suffer, "but only every time." Of course, if you are raising children, teaching them to have good manners and to set good boundaries with others is an exception.

Her model, "The Work" has a basic framework consisting of four questions.

When something stresses you, you ask yourself these questions. It is best not to answer them quickly. If you have the time, quietly sit with them and allow the answers to emerge from the Essential Self and into your conscience mind.

First, identify what the stress is, for example, "Bob shouldn't be rude." Then ask yourself these questions:

1. "Is it true? (Yes or no. If no, move to question 3.)
2. Can you absolutely know that it's true?
3. How do you react, what happens, when you believe that thought?
4. Who would you be without the thought?"

These four questions are followed by "Turnarounds," which are a bit too complex to do justice with here, but are some of the most powerful aspects of this framework.

"The Work" strongly taps into identifying our truths about any stresses or strains we are experiencing. By utilizing this practice on an ongoing basis, the saying "and the truth shall set you free" comes alive.

This model also beautifully dovetails with the practices, techniques, and readings, described in the coming chapters that help us improve the functioning of our brain.

The website for this framework is: *www.thework.com* or *www. byronkatie.com.*

One of the great things about Katie's work is that the staff offers free assistance to anyone who calls in on the phone and is trying to utilize these four questions and turnarounds on a problem. My experience is the staff are well trained, skilled, and very helpful.

Overall, "The Work" can be an extremely helpful tool for finding our way back to the Essential Self, and can be utilized anywhere, anytime, and in almost any situation.

If you are like most people, you may find yourself sometimes bristling at the question "Is it true?" For example, is it true that people shouldn't be rude? My personality wants to scream, "YES! THIS IS TRUE!" Yet when I quietly sit with the question, and allow a deeper truth to surface, I may get a different answer. You may find that sometimes you just don't want to give in; you may feel the need to hold onto the way you want things to be. So, when you get jammed, ask yourself.

Which would I prefer, to be right or to be free?

On the other hand, if a thought or belief seems true to you, go with that.

Third Framework: The Sedona Method

This was developed by physicist Lester Levenson in the 1950's, which he later formulated into a training method through the Sedona Institute. Hale Dwoskin took over after Mr. Levenson died, and substantially broadened the availability of this model. It can now also be accessed through his book *The Sedona Method* by Hale Dwoskin. The website is *www.sedona.com*. The essence of this model is three questions a person can ask themselves at any time. The questions are about wanting control, approval, or to feel safe.

Years ago, Mr. Levenson explained to me the basis for the Sedona Method. It seemed theoretically sound to me, and I derived great benefit from it for many years. He formulated that at our earliest stages of life, we want to survive. We quickly learn that in order to do that, we try to keep our parents' love and approval so that they will take good care of us, thereby ensuring our survival. As we get a little older, we desire to have our own way more often but don't want to lose our parents' love and approval. Therefore, we learn to control people and situations so that we can have our own way more often, yet not lose their approval.

Over time, these desires for wanting control, wanting approval, and wanting to feel safe build up layer upon layer. By asking ourselves certain questions whenever we feel stressed, or that something is not right, we can unravel these layers that have covered up our Essence for most of our lives.

Just as with the first two models described previously, this model can be utilized anytime or anyplace, and clearly facilitates our reengaging with our Essential Self.

Fourth Framework: Recovery International

I just learned about this model a few years ago. As a psychiatrist who has been on this path for many years, I thought I was at least aware of most everything out there that addresses the reclaiming of our Essential Self. As I discovered this to be a very effective method, I also found that hardly anyone seemed to know about it.

The name of the organization is Recovery International (originally called Recovery, Inc.), and it has been in business for about sixty years. I have read their books and attended a number of their group meetings. I also know people who have been utilizing these practices on a daily basis for several years, and have made remarkable strides in reconnecting with their Essential Self.

This approach was formulated by a psychiatrist named Abraham A. Low, MD, and was first published in book form in 1950.[13] This was a time when psychoanalysis was extremely popular—and very expensive. Dr. Low formulated this approach so that people could have effective tools for getting past thought, emotional, and behavior patterns that were creating problems in their lives.

Just as the first three models offer an approach that can be utilized anytime and anywhere, so does Recovery International.

The practice is to catch ourselves when we are engaging in thoughts, emotions, or behaviors that cause or reinforce us to have difficulties. We then "spot" ourselves from a list of truth-based statements. This is what they call the technique. The long-term effect of utilizing this approach each day is that our lives become much more truth based. And remember, truth is the underlying aspect of our Essential Self. This approach automatically gives us a much greater sense of resilience to a multitude of stressors that would have previously tipped us over emotionally and/or behaviorally.

My best guess as to why this is not a more popular and well known model may have something to do with the tone of some of Dr. Low's writings. Some people perceive that he sometimes speaks down to clients in his books; this may be related to the fact that they were written at a time when doctors were placed on a pedestal and viewed as all-knowing. While some passages might be difficult reading, I encourage you to get beyond this because, in my opinion, this model is truly excellent and potentially life changing.

Recovery International offers books, workbooks, live support group meetings, and online meetings. You can visit their website at *www.RecoveryInternational.org.*

Fifth Framework: The Twelve Steps[14]

This is an extraordinary model with which most people are familiar or have heard about. Twelve-step programs can also be powerfully utilized in combination with any of the other four framework examples.

If you're thinking *Hey, I'm not an addict! So why would I do a twelve-step program?* you needn't worry and shouldn't discount it because of that. The twelve-step program, in general, cuts right to the quick of the human condition. If you are living from the false self, which most of us do, this framework can be quite valuable. In our modern world, almost all people resort to some type of self-medicating and/or addictive behavior in order to cope with the incredible stresses and strains we are exposed to. It doesn't have to be a substance. We can become addicted to perfectionism, busy-ness, work, shopping, the internet, music, television, sex, gambling, food, tobacco, obsessing, intensity, etc.

For the purposes of this book, working with the Twelve Steps on a daily basis gradually reconnects us with our Essential Self. It can be used anytime or anyplace. It can be practiced concurrent with any of the other four models, which is why I have listed it last.

The Twelve-Step Model addresses cleaning up fight, flight, and freeze stuckness before moving into connecting more deeply with what they call our Higher Power. The equivalent of fight mode is resentments; the equivalent of flight mode is fear; and the equivalent of freeze mode is where we are before stepping into action.

The twelve-step program has been expanded to fit almost any form of self-medication or addiction imaginable! If you still do not think you have *any* forms of self-medication addictions, check out Co-Dependents Anonymous (CoDA) and/or Adult Children of Alcoholics (ACoA). You need not have been raised in an alcoholic family to be helped by ACoA. These two twelve-step programs often address the most basic type of human suffering: what happens when we give our center and power over to anything other than the truth of who/what we are. They show us how to correct this faulty pattern.

Twelve-step programs often have live, online, and phone meetings, literature, sponsors, and a number of printed materials, videos, and audios. There are a very wide variety of twelve-step meetings, and each is somewhat different. I usually recommend people try out several different meetings until settling on one that feels most comfortable. Similarly, you can attend meetings that are for addictions you don't even have. The bottom line is still the same. For example, I once lived in a small city that had very little in the way of CoDA meetings, but had wonderful Alcoholics Anonymous meetings, and plenty of them! In my mind, I would just substitute the word alcohol or alcoholic with the challenges I was dealing with at the time.

Some twelve-step meetings are sponsored by religious organizations, but most are not.

Be aware that the quality of twelve-step meetings can vary widely, so don't hesitate to shop around. In general, the meetings that are based on *The Big Book of Alcoholics Anonymous* tend to be the strongest and offer the most healing. Again, even the meetings that address addictions that are not related to alcohol use may use this book as their foundation.

The Way I Utilize These Frameworks/Models

During my twenties, I used the Sedona Method on a daily basis. I derived a lot of benefit from it, but it wasn't until several years later that I began piecing together a winning combination for myself.

In my case, I learned the Byron Katie framework, "The Work." Around the same time, I learned Pia Mellody's model. I found that these two frameworks dovetailed together beautifully. Mellody's method offered an in-depth understanding of the five Core Issues. As I moved out of the extremes of these Core Issues, my experience with my Essential Self directly improved.

I found that "The Work" was a wonderful tool to dig down into my experiences. This enabled me to deepen my work with Pia Mellody's model much more quickly. For me, they synergized with each other.

Several years later, I began to see the incredible power and healing offered by a strong twelve-step program when integrated with the other two frameworks I was using. The twelve-step model offered practical and detailed guidance for spiritual fitness that ultimately synergized with "The Work" and Pia Mellody's frameworks.

Additionally, my childhood had been riddled with significant psychological trauma. I have intermittently added practices and techniques from the next three chapters to my personal process. Eye Movement Desensitization and Reprocessing (EMDR) was particularly useful for clearing out deep blocks that could not be transcended with the aforementioned frameworks. In turn, EMDR cleared the way for the frameworks to be more effective. Over the years, many of my patients, friends, and relatives have identified different combinations of frameworks, or just one. Each of our minds is unique, meaning that finding our own path may be helpful. Again, professional guidance may assist us in making our choices.

Many people who are chronically "amped up" in a flight or fight baseline (too anxious, too angry, constantly waiting for the other shoe to drop, too shut down, etc.) may need to start by calming the limbic areas and brainstem with practices and techniques in the chapter "Calling Off the Dogs!" before aforementioned frameworks can help much. However, it is also not unusual that people can really take off and progress with just a framework or two. Therefore, there is no sure way to know ahead of time what game plan will work best for each person.

If someone begins working with a framework, and then waits to see how their experience connecting with their Essential Self does or doesn't evolve, they may consider adding to their efforts practices and interventions from the following three chapters. Listed are a wide variety of options, so consulting with a professional first is important.

Chapter 9

Calling Off the Dogs!

W e have looked at getting stabilized—for those who need or want it—and choosing one or two frameworks to help us get on track of our desired life path.

This chapter addresses ways of quieting chronic fight, flight, and freeze energy that is generated and locked into place by the ancient survival brain areas; the limbic areas, and brainstem. For many people, this may be a needed step before they can fully engage with a framework. For others, it may only be needed if somewhere down the line they become stuck. And still for others, these "Calling Off the Dogs" practices and techniques may not be needed at all. Finally, many people find utilizing some of these practices and techniques as very enriching for their path, whether or not they "need" it.

Let's begin by reviewing some of the elements that entrap our attention and experience in the ancient survival parts of our brain.

1. The unconscious emotional valence attached to people, experiences, and perceptions usually pulls our attention away from our Essential Self. "Valence" is the degree of charge something or someone has on our emotions and bodies, both positive and negative. The valence associated with the Essential Self is *initially* quite low, and we barely even notice it. But as we come to recognize it and align with it more, the valence can markedly increase.

2. The unconscious fight, flight, or freeze complexes that play back virtually as if they are real (but we are not in actual life threatening circumstances), and as if they are in the here and now, but are not.

3. The chronic states of fight, flight, or freeze that continually hijack our attention away from our Essential Self. Our nervous system actually becomes amped up or down on an ongoing basis because of these stress responses created in childhood.

4. Our attention turns more and more away from our Essential Self and becomes fixated on what's outside of us. By the time we are older children or adolescents, we have long forgotten the experience of our true nature, our core self.

5. Many of these fight, flight, or freeze responses have become locked together with a perception or belief that then becomes a Deep False Belief. Expectations naturally flow from these erroneous convictions. Over the years, we accumulate enough of these that they ultimately become our identity.

6. Habits are created by all of this conditioning, which further place us on autopilot within our false self.

Remember, we can't be stuck in our survival brain areas and connect with our Essential Self at the same time. How do we find our way back? We *relax* into our Essential Self. We don't earn it, learn it, buy it, grow into it, or achieve it.

We relax into our Essential Self. We don't earn it, learn it, buy it, grow into it, or achieve it.

Peace is an inherent quality of our true or core self. That which does not come from a place of peace cannot easily resonate with it. Our false self that developed as a means to keep us safe is not based upon peace; it is based upon fear.

Peace is an inherent quality of our true or core self. That which does not come from a place of peace cannot easily resonate with it. Our false self that developed as a means to keep us safe is not based upon peace; it is based upon fear.

As described earlier, our underlying baseline of subtle, yet powerfully strong fear (whether we can consciously see it or not), is generated from our ancient survival brain areas. These circuits have retained the dominant power over almost all other brain circuits for many millions of years. They are the alpha dog of the brain. They can override almost anything. They are in charge—that is, until we train them to play second fiddle to our Essential Self. The exceptions, of course, include when these brain areas really are protecting us from real threats.

Remember, that when our fight, flight, and freeze responses are firing, for seconds at a time, all the way up to ongoing for many years, our prefrontal cortex goes offline to varying degrees. If we're stuck in crisis mode (that is chronic fight, flight, and freeze, which many adults are to one degree or another), our prefrontal cortex is chronically offline. It is our prefrontal cortex and some other cortical areas of the brain that enable us to be present in the here and now, if the survival brain areas are calm. *If we work on these ancient survival brain areas initially, our prefrontal cortex and other cortical areas become more available to us so we can work with them as tools for having what we want.*

Mindfulness meditation, for example, is proving to be extremely helpful for calming and retraining some of the ancient survival brain areas. But the areas of the brain where mindfulness practices work are mainly in areas of the prefrontal cortex and related areas, and so are offline when we are in temporary or chronic fight, flight, or freeze mode. Many people who are stuck with too many fight, flight, or freeze complexes are not yet able to sit still long enough or quietly enough to meditate. They may have to begin with other approaches. At some point, when their ancient survival brain areas are calm enough, beginning to practice mindfulness meditation can be extremely helpful.

Similarly, other techniques and practices that are related mainly to the prefrontal cortex may be limited in their value until the prefrontal cortex comes back online.

Therefore, we may want to begin with a practice such as yoga. This can strengthen some of the same brain areas that will ultimately calm the ancient survival parts of the brain. We don't have to sit quietly to practice yoga. With traditional yoga, the same strong element of mindfulness is present, but without having to sit still. It is the element of mindfulness that can strongly calm the ancient survival brain areas. By the way, I don't mean hot yoga or yoga while hanging from a helicopter! I mean regular, slow, mindful, non-intense forms of yoga. The extreme forms of yoga can actually activate the limbic brain areas rather than calm them. (The extreme forms of almost everything can activate the limbic brain.)

David, whom we read about earlier, is a good example. As he goes through his life in chronic states of fight mode, which is chronic anger, this reflects that areas of his limbic brain are too active at their baseline. There is a good chance that David would have difficulty, at least initially, in sitting still and being quiet enough to engage in mindfulness meditation. But he would probably have little difficulty with yoga practices or certain martial arts, like Tai Chi. Once his limbic brain areas settle enough, he could probably gain much from mindfulness meditation and other mindfulness practices. In turn, it may become easier for David to reconnect with his Essential Self.

It is so common in human beings to be inundated and log-jammed with fight, flight, and freeze complexes, that it feels like who we are. But this is not true. Our underlying nature, or the Essential Self, is not in a chronic state of fight, flight, or freeze.

I'm frequently asked if someone can be in more than one of these stressful states. Yes! Most adults have layer upon layer of fight, flight, and freeze complexes. Most children start out with perhaps one layer, but then, over the years, most of us develop more and more, like the layers of an onion. That's why children who receive certain kinds of very effective treatment for too much unprocessed fight, flight, or freeze, such as eye movement desensitization and reprocessing (EMDR), typically respond much more quickly than adults, as there is less to clean out. When the backlogged, unprocessed fight, flight, and freeze complexes are cleaned out, the Essential Self is right there. This is usually quickly evident with children. (However, if children receive treatment interventions that don't address these fight/flight/freeze complexes, this source that causes them discomfort can go on for a long time.) I've seen many well-intentioned professionals utilizing mainly talking therapies for young children, which often don't seem to help much with the fight, flight, freeze complexes in the ancient survival brain areas.

One of the best ways of opening a door to access our Essential Self is by quieting down these chronic states of fight, flight, or freeze.

One of the best ways of opening a door to access our Essential Self is by quieting down these chronic states of fight, flight, or freeze. Doing this kind of work, which quiets the limbic system and helps the brainstem get better regulated, is what I call the Calling Off the Dogs for reclaiming our Essential Self. Not only does our true essence become more evident, but our whole system—body, emotions, and mind—can become much more relaxed.

The same holds true for accessing many needed functions of our prefrontal cortex and other cortical areas. We just can't access them adequately when the fight, flight, or freeze virtual tapes play over and over again in the ancient survival brain areas.

One more point before we look at actual practices and techniques: you may notice that there is not much talking/understanding therapy listed in this chapter, e.g., psychodynamic psychotherapy, supportive therapy, cognitive behavioral therapy, etc. As mentioned earlier, this is mainly because the prefrontal cortex is relatively offline when areas of the limbic brain and brainstem are overactivated. The main part of the brain that is engaged during talking/understanding therapy is the prefrontal cortex. Therefore, for many people, it's more challenging to successfully utilize the talking/understanding interventions at the beginning. Once the ancient survival brain areas quiet down, that's often when we can derive much more benefit from the talking interventions. And again, the talking interventions do not tend to quiet down the lower brain areas very effectively.

David, for example, may initially not benefit much from standard "talk therapy." His anger at authority figures is heavily in his limbic brain, and the fight-complexes are locked into his limbic brain and brainstem areas. Again, the standard talk therapies would not enable much access to these brain areas, at least initially.

How to "Call Off the Dogs"

Let's break down these different approaches into three categories. The first are techniques and/or practices that are designed for people to use on their own.

The second are techniques that can be used by people on their own, after varying amounts of initial training with a professional.

The third are techniques that generally require a professional throughout the process. Please note that there are many other interventions, books, etc., that are not listed here, as they are too numerous to mention. I am including the ones with which I am most familiar. Also, as mentioned earlier, some people are able to reconnect with their Essential Self with just the use of a daily framework. Calling Off the Dogs may or may not offer additional help.

Self-Help*

This is a partial listing of potential self-help techniques and practices, and they are in no particular order:

Mindfulness Practices

These are a group of practices that have a common theme of calmly noticing and welcoming either thoughts, emotions, or sensations in the body as they occur. This process is called mindfulness. Many people think of mindfulness as only meditation,

---

* The following information is not intended to replace treatment recommended by a mental health provider. For any kind of mental health history or problems, or if you don't know, check with a professional first before beginning this process.

but mindfulness practices also include movement, like yoga, Tai Chi, or others.

Yoga can help settle the limbic brain enough that a person can begin to sit quietly without too much agitation. There are other mindfulness practices that you can explore. A great place to start is by attending actual classes for mindfulness training, or exploring CDs from practitioners such as Jon Kabat-Zinn, Tara Brach, Thich Nhat Hanh, Jack Kornfield, Shinzen Young, and others.[15, 16, 17, 18, 19]

Recovery International Groups, Books, and Workbooks

This is one of the five frameworks/models that we looked at in the last chapter. However, this can also be utilized as an intervention for "Calling Off the Dogs."

It can be very helpful if practiced regularly. This approach both retrains the limbic brain to quiet down and connects us to our Essential Self. Aside from the purchase of a few books, it's free. There are phone and online meetings and actual group meetings around the world that are a good place to begin practicing these techniques. For information, see *www.recoveryinternational.org*.

Emotional Freedom Technique (EFT) or tapping

This simple technique has several steps to it, which include tapping on certain energy meridian points on the face, hands, and upper torso. It can be very effective in calming survival areas of the brain and it's been around for years. The more regularly it is practiced, the greater the effect.[20] It only takes a few minutes to use and can be practiced anywhere and anytime. The founder is Gary Craig, and the website address is *www.emofree.com.*

Yoga

Yoga practice is a really "heavy hitter" with all three areas of the brain. It has the potential to be very helpful in at least three ways. It can calm the survival limbic areas, help to regulate the brainstem, and strengthen areas of the cortex. But be cautious that there are some types of yoga that are quite intense and might defeat your purpose. For example, doing yoga in a very hot room, or doing it quickly, or without enough mindfulness, may have other benefits, but probably won't help as much with these brain areas. *Overcoming Trauma Through Yoga*, by David Emerson and Elizabeth Hopper, is a wonderful book that explains how to approach yoga as a means to settle these parts of the brain.[21]

Tai Chi and Qigong

When it comes to positive brain effects, these ancient Chinese practices are very similar to yoga. They combine elements of mindfulness with slow, methodical movements, and breathing exercises. As with yoga, many people can gain physical benefits from these low-impact exercises.

EmWave Device and Software

When the brainstem becomes chronically dysregulated, it often throws off our whole game. We just don't feel comfortable in our skin. The HeartMath company[22] has been developing and improving both their hand-held EmWave device, and their computer software for many years. If practiced regularly, this can gradually help the brainstem's regulation improve. Without getting too technical, there is a function in our brainstem called *heart rate coherence,* that when working well, gives us a sense of well-being. This opens the door to reconnect with our Essential Self. Our degree of heart rate coherence reflects how well our brainstem is regulated. This is probably the single most important measurement for assessing the overall wellness and intactness of a person's autonomic nervous system (from where the fight/flight/freeze responses originate). This device and/or the computer software not only measure someone's baseline heart rate coherence, but also trains the person into better and better heart rate coherence. Their website is *www.heartmath.com.*

Breath Work

Breathing in certain patterns can strongly influence the brainstem. Inhaling for a certain count, then holding the breath for a certain count, and then exhaling for a certain count is the general way this is done. The trick here is to do it in a way that is helpful for you. A CD by Dr. Andrew Weil called *Breathing: The Master Key to Healing,*[23] can train you in this direction. This is not a practice you would want to do without training from Dr. Weil's CD, or a professional, as breath work can also be done in a harmful manner. Most people initially

Our breathing is our only faculty that has profound influence on our overall state of well-being, and that can be under our conscious control.

think that because we breathe all the time, breath work isn't all that helpful. This is just not accurate; there is much potential healing from this. Our breathing is our only faculty that has profound influence on our overall state of well-being, and that can be under our conscious control.

Practicing Stillness

After the survival parts of the brain are significantly quieted down, and you can comfortably maintain inner quiet, waves of stillness may come upon you, which can be very enjoyable. This is great! Stillness is a manifestation of the Essential Self. But this cannot be a forced stillness. If you force it, it may just be another "should." As we looked at earlier, shoulds come from a completely different brain area.

"The Work" Technique by Byron Katie

"The Work" was also one of the framework/models described earlier. However, we can also use it as a technique for quieting the limbic and brainstem areas, if we don't want to use it as a framework. Again their website is: *www.thework.com*.

Breaking Free of Habits

It is important to identify the layers of habits, which are really just forms of conditioning, that lock us into automatic ways of thinking, behaving, and reacting, and then prevent them from building back up again. Habits become partially locked in through the brainstem level as procedural memories. One of the best approaches I have seen for systematically identifying and clearing habits that get in the way of having what's most important to us, is explained in a small book called *One Small Step Can Change Your Life: The Kaizen Way* by Robert Maurer, PhD. Another great book for this is *The Power of Habit* by Charles Duhigg.[24, 25]

Twelve-Step Programs

This was previously described as one of the frameworks, but can also be used on a more intermittent basis to Call Off the Dogs.

Exercise

Research has repeatedly shown the benefits that regular physical exercise offers in improving brain regulation and relieving stress.[26, 27] We don't need to run out and join a gym or dive into training for a marathon. Something as simple as strapping on our sneakers and heading outside for a walk can work wonders. In general, exercise can reduce our stress levels, but it does not specifically Call Off the Dogs.

Can we mix and match some of these practices? Often yes, but with a few caveats: be cautious to avoid habits of intensity or extremeness. In other words, don't do anything to the extreme on an ongoing basis. Remember what Emerson said: *Moderation in all things!* When we are not moderate and become too intense or extreme, we tend to lose connection with our Essential Self.

Intensity is often glorified in our culture so it is not surprising to think that "faster," "more difficult," and "more often" are better. While there are certain instances where this is true, we shouldn't think we need to keep the switch on high all the time. Be aware that intensity just reactivates the survival brain areas all over again, so we should keep this in mind as we piece together a Game Plan.

Also, until you become more familiar with these, check with a professional—at least initially—to figure out which ones you may want to mix-and-match.

Techniques and Practices That
May Be Used by People on Their Own,
After Working with a Professional

Dialectical Behavior Therapy (DBT)[28, 29]

This is a technique that is initially taught with a group of people, or individually, by a trained DBT therapist. Once someone gets the hang of it, they can apply it to many situations and interactions, reflecting on their own thought processes, etc., outside of the therapy sessions. This technique was originally created for people with certain personality disorders; however, I have seen this technique be very helpful to most people whose thinking and emotions create chronic stress in themselves.

IMPACT[30]

At this time, this training is only offered in Boston. Hopefully, it will expand to other cities. Founded by Meg Stone, this is for people who have become traumatized from assault and similar traumas, and is a wonderful hands-on short training that can be utilized for the rest of a person's life. IMPACT also organizes many workshops. For more information, visit *www.Impact Boston.com.*

Cranial Electrotherapy Stimulation (CES) [31, 32, 33]

This is a device that has been FDA-approved and on the market since the 1970s. It is generally considered safe if utilized correctly and you have ongoing supervision by a trained professional. It has two clips that simply attach to the earlobes, and can be set to various settings. A gentle electrical current gradually trains certain brain areas to function within more normal parameters. Overall, this device has received very positive reviews for helping people with depression, anxiety, some sleep problems, easing withdrawal from certain addictions, and many other problems. Much of what it does is calm and help better regulate the limbic and brainstem areas.

Somatic Experiencing™ [35]

This is a wonderful, helpful group of techniques developed by Dr. Peter Levine. Somatic Experiencing significantly helps the brainstem become more regulated, and calms the limbic area— the two main parts of the ancient survival brain areas—and integrates these changes with the person's everyday functioning. After several sessions with a Somatic Experiencing therapist, many people are able to carry out at least some of these techniques on their own. However, confer with your Somatic Experiencing therapist before doing this. For more information, visit the website *www.TraumaHealing.org.*

Techniques and Practices
That Require Professional Guidance

Eye Movement Desensitization and Reprocessing (EMDR)

Founded by Dr. Francine Shapiro in the early nineties, this is an extremely effective treatment for clearing out the fight, flight, freeze complexes, clearing out Deep False Beliefs, and clearing out expectations of ourselves and others. This therapy helps to stabilize all three brain levels. In a nutshell, this technique involves the therapist identifying at the deepest possible level what the *negative cognition* is that is locking the person into suffering. (This "negative cognition" has some similarities to Deep False Beliefs.) A form of alternating bilateral stimulation is utilized —such as an EMDR light bar (a horizontal bar with a line of lights that alternately flash to the right and left, that the person follows with their eyes), tapping, or sounds over a headset—to dissolve the fight, flight, freeze complexes.

Dr. Shapiro had the wisdom to subject her technique to ongoing research, and therefore a large amount of evidence supporting the effectiveness of this therapy. As indicated, this is not a treatment you can do on your own. The two main websites to learn more about it are *www.EMDR.com* and *www.EMDRIA.org.* There are fully trained EMDR clinicians all over the world.

This is the main technique that I have been using in my private practice for many years.[34]

Neurofeedback

Neurofeedback has been around for many years, but has primarily been utilized for attention deficit disorder (ADD) and other related disorders. In the past several years, however, it has also been found to be potentially very helpful in treating many different disorders, including depression, anxiety, some sleep problems, post-traumatic stress disorder (PTSD)[36] and more. What is wonderful about this technique is that it can help to stabilize the brain's electrical activity relatively quickly, including the survival brain areas. This can potentially enable people to accelerate the process of calming the ancient survival parts of the brain, and empowering some of the cortical areas. It's a form of biofeedback that is used with brainwaves. Very briefly, a person's baseline brainwaves are measured. The neurofeedback therapist then programs a computer to maximize the chance that the person's brainwaves will begin to shift more toward normal. Nothing is put into the person's brain! (This is a common misunderstanding.) A few electrodes are glued to the scalp, which take ongoing measurements of the brainwaves throughout the session. The client watches the computer monitor, which is either showing a game or some type of picture. The game will only proceed when the person's brain waves are conforming closer to normal. These sessions are usually experienced as pleasurable, yet potentially profound healing is taking place within the brain's electrical patterns. Because it is both efficient and effective, it is my sense that this technique may become a leader in this field.

There are several neurofeedback training companies, each a little different from the other. I am most familiar with the EEGER[37] model (*www.EEGER.com*). However, regardless of which training a clinician has received, there is an overarching certification board called Biofeedback Certification International Alliance, or BCIA. Clinicians who specialize in neurofeedback and qualify for BCIA certification are listed as "BCN" in the "Find a Clinician" section of the BCIA website, *www.BCIA.org*. (Be careful not to choose someone with only the "BCB" designation as this is for biofeedback, not neurofeedback.)

Internal Family Systems (IFS)

Founded by Dr. Richard Schwartz many years ago, I've found this to be a very powerful therapeutic technique for Calling Off the Dogs and strengthening other brain areas. Don't let the name fool you—this is *not* family therapy! It is my observation that it helps to stabilize all three brain levels from the effects of the ancient survival brain areas being overactive or underactive. This is a type of therapy that utilizes visual imagery that comes from the client's own mind but is facilitated by the therapist. Visit *www.SelfLeadership.org* to learn more.

Acupuncture

This is a treatment that has been around for thousands of years. Acupuncture uses very thin needles to stimulate specific points in the body to allow blocked energy (*chi*) to flow freely in order to relieve a wide variety of distress and promote self-healing. It can potentially be very helpful in stabilizing overactive and underactive ancient survival brain areas. In my opinion, the trick is to find a good acupuncturist. Many Westerners have taken acupuncture training for weeks to a few years, but they often don't have the same level of skill as many of the Eastern practitioners who were raised with it and have trained with it for many years. Of course, there are many exceptions.

Medications

I'm often asked about utilizing psychiatric medications to help stabilize the survival brain areas. I can only share with you my particular bias. For severe psychiatric problems, I perceive medications as potentially being a godsend to many people. For example, medication can be very valuable for people with severe depression, severe anxiety or panic disorders; bipolar disorder type 1 and many cases of type 2; obsessive compulsive disorder, any of the psychotic disorders, such as schizophrenia, and a number of other disorders. In these kinds of cases, I perceive these medications as potentially giving people a new lease on life.

For people with mild symptoms, if they are interested, their symptoms can often be utilized as a barometer of how they are progressing with these other practices and/or therapies. Remember that the closer one lives his or her life aligned with the Essential Self, the better they feel. The more one has turned away from their Essential Self, the more they suffer. This suffering can be in the form of emotional symptoms, physical symptoms, and feeling uncomfortable in one's own skin.

As mentioned earlier, I recently came upon this statistic in a few different places, including *The New York Times:* approximately 25 percent of American women in their forties and fifties are taking antidepressant medication![38] My educated guess would be that many of these women who do not have the more severe forms of depression, may derive benefit by calming certain areas of their brain and strengthening others, and may not need medication treatment.

Some people with severe, recurrent depression may need to continue with medication indefinitely. Again, it's wise to consult with a healthcare provider when considering any changes in treatment.

Key Points

1. A great help for many people in reconnecting with their Essential Self is calming the overactive ancient survival brain areas. This enables certain other parts of the brain to become more active, which is more conducive for reconnecting with the Essential Self.

2. There are many possible ways to help calm the ancient survival brain areas. Several of these are described above and in other chapters.

3. Remember, we can't be stuck in the survival parts of our brain and connect with our Essential Self at the same time.

Principle of Essential Living

- *Our brain contains ancient circuits that block access to our Essential Self. Reconnecting with our Essential Self may be facilitated by quieting and calming these ancient circuits.*

Chapter 10

Free the Hostages

After using some of the frameworks and techniques in previous chapters, many people feel so much better that they don't want to go any further. However, if you're interested in reconnecting even more with the Essential Self, read on! The next step can help you deepen a reconnection through empowering certain cortical areas of the brain, that is, the outer layer, which is also the evolutionarily newest area of the brain.

This chapter is about freeing and strengthening the prefrontal cortex, which has been pulled offline from too much fight, flight, or freeze activity.

As people increasingly grow calmer and retrain the ancient brain survival areas, the prefrontal cortex increasingly returns online and the Essential Self increasingly reveals itself. Therefore, any other techniques that people can undertake that heavily involve the thinking brain areas will now be much easier to utilize and, accordingly, may reap richer results.

In addition, as the prefrontal cortex functions begin improving, our own personal understanding of things—*knowing who we are and are not*, figuring out solutions to problems, more accurately understanding things (with much less emotional overlay)—may begin to blossom! Look at the list on page 201 to see some of the functions of the prefrontal cortex. *These areas can improve when we Call Off the Dogs, and empower the cortical and other areas of our brain!*

Concerning interventions for reconnecting with the Essential Self, as mentioned earlier, many of these just don't work as well if you use them *before* the ancient survival brain areas let go of their tight grip on the prefrontal cortex and some other cortical areas. In general, it's an uphill battle to utilize prefrontal cortex interventions before the prefrontal cortex areas are released from being offline. It's like trying to make yourself do a complicated Sudoku or crossword puzzle when you're seriously sleep deprived—it's terribly challenging.

Interventions like talking therapies, supportive psychotherapy, cognitive behavioral therapy, Sedona Method, thought stopping, and many others can be remarkably powerful aids. However, it's been my observation that these and many other interventions are at their most valuable when the person's ancient survival brain areas are already calmed to some degree. Otherwise, that chronic state of fight, flight, freeze can be challenging to override.

At some point, which may be different for each person, these chronic states of fight, flight, and freeze relent enough that the "lights" of the prefrontal cortex turn on again, in other words, the prefrontal cortex is back online. A vast range of functions become increasingly available. And, as the prefrontal cortex becomes more and more functional, the ancient survival brain areas quiet even more. This, in turn, has a domino effect, freeing up the prefrontal cortex even more, which enables the ancient survival brain areas to relax even more.

Don is a fifty-year-old, high-level executive. He came to me for EMDR treatment for bothersome ongoing anxiety about getting certain major work projects completed. He had been struggling with this problem for years, but always managed to pull it off in time for the deadline. Now, however, he had met his match! He needed to produce a new program, and implement it company-wide, including presenting to a number of high-level executives. Don had always experienced the presentation part of his job as very intimidating. He had already tried various kinds of interventions on his own, and another intervention with a cognitive behavioral therapist, and only felt about 20 to 30 percent more capable of tackling the task at hand.

Using EMDR, we cleared out the early origins of the fight, flight, freeze complexes that were chronically playing back the virtual tapes of "I just can't do this!" Don had felt this sense strongly in his emotions and body for years whenever these types of work projects had come up.

After he cleared these out of the ancient survival brain areas over the course of five sessions, he successfully flew through the project and its implementation. Along the way, he intermittently felt some self-doubt. However, now he could easily and successfully utilize some of the same techniques that had done little for him prior to quieting his ancient survival brain areas.

One of the interventions he was using is what I call a "Thought Throw-Out Box." This is a type of thought-stopping technique that we will look at more closely later. This is a very simple technique where a relatively small box, with an index-card-sized slot on top with the words "Throw-Out Thoughts" written on it, is used along with a stack of blank index cards. Whenever a negative thought about his not being able to successfully complete a project would arise, that was Don's signal to take out a fresh index card, write down the negative thought, and ask himself if the thought was true or false. If he discerned that it wasn't true, he would discard the index card into the box, while acknowledging to himself that the thought just wasn't true. He would then visualize himself completely letting go of the thought. This process tended to be quite pleasant for Don.

Again, this deceptively simple technique did little to nothing for him prior to calling off the dogs (in this case, EMDR), but was an instant "vacuum cleaner" once he quieted down the overactive survival brain areas.

I have seen many patients over the years who have come to me after trying medication, and then various types of cognitive behavioral therapy for problems with chronic anxiety. Most of them reported that the medication usually helped significantly, but only while they were taking it; the symptoms worsened again when the medications were decreased and/or stopped. They wanted a more permanent fix than that. With cognitive-behavioral therapies, patients reported some improvement in their symptoms, but still had ongoing or intermittent anxiety that significantly disturbed and/or limited their daily lives. The symptoms were mainly described as the bodily and emotional equivalents of being in a state of chronic flight. Their *thought processes* had been aided by the cognitive-behavioral therapy, but their bodily and emotional symptoms from too much fight, flight, freeze were only somewhat improved. Approaches like EMDR, neurofeedback, and Somatic Experiencing described earlier, are usually more effective at this.

Can you see how what we looked at earlier applies here? Our ancient survival brain areas evolved millions and millions of years prior to our thinking brains. The fight, flight, and freeze responses work significantly independently of our thought processes, and exert their influence mainly on the body and emotions. Our thought processes are secondarily affected because they are pulled offline. The cognitive-behavioral therapies tend to focus upon clearing irrational thoughts that trigger these fight, flight, freeze responses. But to the degree that we have a backlog of fight, flight, and/or freeze complexes already locked within our brains, this approach may have more limited effects until more of the fight, flight, freeze complexes are cleared out or calmed by approaches described in the last chapter.

That is why in Don's case the deceptively simple thought throw-out box worked so well; enough of the fight, flight, freeze complex had been cleared through EMDR first. Don was left with very clear discernment that he, in fact, could very successfully complete this major project, and could easily throw out the thoughts that told him otherwise. His prefrontal cortex was now clearly in charge. When he initially tried this technique and others prior to EMDR, his ancient survival brain areas were in charge, and the thinking brain had little power in his situation.

The only way to know for sure if someone has too much of a fight, flight, or freeze logjam that would prevent them from successfully using interventions that utilize the prefrontal cortex is to try them. If the results are nil or equivocal, that person may need to begin with Calling Off the Dogs. Again, one should first consult with a skilled professional.

Make no mistake—even after someone makes good progress, if and when our ancient survival brain areas develop fight, flight, freeze complexes about anything, they will very likely "bury" our prefrontal cortex functioning. Our clear thinking remains at the mercy of the ancient survival brain areas.

In my experience with EMDR, after people work through what they initially entered treatment for, they may come back later for other issues that arise, but these "tune-ups" tend to be shorter than the initial treatment. The person and their brain understand that, "This is not about me; this is about some fight, flight, freeze complexes that are getting in my way." It's no longer perceived as a personal weakness or flaw. It's just like when you go to the dentist for a cavity. The cavity has nothing to do with you or your worth; it's just a cavity, a hole in your tooth that needs to be cleaned out and filled so you can get back to your life.

- *Paying attention, observing, analyzing, organizing, logic, basic understanding, sense of time, planning, anticipating.*

- *Representational memory, the "story" of our lives, personality.*

- *Impulse control, inhibiting actions that are not appropriate, some emotional regulation, self-control.*

- *The context of an experience, some of our social skills, ability to mediate, negotiate, and weigh possible judgments.*

- *Empathy, ethics, morality, wisdom, personal will, intentions.*

- *Higher Consciousness: access to a sense of joy, peace, love, acceptance (not resignation), sense of oneness, serenity, equanimity, even-mindedness, sense of "all is well" (even if it is not), altruism (but not when it is from a "should"), ability to surrender to something greater than ourselves, gratitude, etc.*

Figure 13. Some Functions of the Prefrontal Cortex in Humans.

In a similar vein, as folks become more adept at clearing out
Deep False Beliefs from childhood and chronic fight, flight, and
freeze complexes, it becomes easier and easier to identify that
which is not me or true for me. Once we see it, it usually lessens
or disappears.

The three principles below are aspects of the prefrontal cortex, and other areas, that are functioning at their highest levels.

1. One of the most powerful things we can ultimately
   do in our lives is keep clarifying more deeply what is
   most important to us. Can it change? Sure! As we gain
   clarity in our thinking, and greater calm in our body,
   what we identify as most important may become more
   and more clear over time. In our culture, we are used
   to obtaining our answers through only our thinking.
   A huge addition to the accuracy of our thinking when
   considering our life's path is to include what a *calm*
   body relates to us. Why? One reason is that the body
   can reflect to us how our deeper brain and Essential
   Self are reading a situation. Bodily input tends to be
   powerfully accurate.

2. As we gradually gain clarity, we should align our lives
   with it. Our decisions, attitudes, and behavior should
   ideally flow from this truth. Conversely, to the best of
   our ability, we should stop whatever is blocking this
   aligning process.

   This makes all the difference between simply

understanding something versus "getting it" at a feeling and "felt sense" level.

3. We shouldn't give our power away. Recognizing and then honoring what is most important for us is probably the most important thing we can do in our lives. There are myriad ways we can short-circuit this process, such as addictions, poor self-care, wanting to get or keep others' approval, not trusting ourselves, and many other items.

When we practice the above as often as possible, we see our life's direction increasingly shift toward a life directed by the Essential Self, thereby increasing our sense of peace, freedom, love, joy, and connectedness.

For many years before writing this book, I would sit down on my birthday and New Year's and as completely and deeply as possible focus upon what was truly most important to me. After I had refined each of my answers until I felt they captured my innermost sense, I made a list of how I could better adapt my life to support whatever I had come up with. The reason I am sharing this with you is because this process is one of the most powerful things you can do! My awakening to the truth of who I am went at least a bit deeper twice each year. Aligning my life with what was true for me made an even more powerful declaration that transcended my ancient survival brain areas' fight, flight, freeze messages.

The process of seeking our true identity, and then aligning our life with it, takes courage. It is not for the meek. The process of identifying what is true or not true for us may challenge some of our deepest conditioning or programming. For example, some of our strongest and most deeply seated ancient survival brain wiring that is present since we were very young children is about keeping our caregivers' approval. This is of prime importance for all mammals! We simply don't survive as young offspring if we don't keep their approval. When we begin to look at what is true or not true for us, we are stepping up to the plate of owning our own lives. Ancient survival programming may be threatened by that, and throw us additional fight, flight, and/or freeze responses and/or complexes. It is wired to fire like crazy if we threaten the status quo of keeping others' approval. You've got to mean business if you're serious about reclaiming your Essential Self.

One of the bottom-line questions we have to ask ourselves, similar to what we mentioned earlier, when we become challenged is: *What do I want more: peace (or freedom, etc.) or approval from others?*

Take the example of Mary, my eighty-three-year-old great-aunt. She's a very nice woman and enjoys excellent health. Over the years, I have watched how she deals with a large variety of challenging situations. When things go wrong, she initially reacts appropriately. For example, if a repairman cuts significant corners on the work he does for her, she becomes aggravated. If a physician makes a mistake, or does not spend adequate time with her to correctly diagnose her, she becomes aggravated. However, she does not follow through with any kind of action or response to rectify the problem. She becomes frozen (fear) when it comes to acting on her truth, and then moves her attention away from it, and tries to forget about it.

For Mary and many others, the answer to the above question is that they want approval from people more than they want peace—or other qualities of the Essential Self. Mary much prefers to be perceived by others as "nice" instead of reclaiming her Essential Self. Is there anything wrong with this? No, not at all. As mentioned before, it is wise to honor wherever you are in your life. When you ask yourself that question: *What do I want more: peace (or freedom, etc.) or approval from others?* Honor your answer.

Mary could very possibly stand up more for her truth if some of the load of the powerful and ancient chronic flight and freeze lessened.

What is probably the biggest enemy to most people on their path to reconnecting with their Essential Self? It is their identifying with their negative thoughts (e.g., *I am stupid*), or limiting thoughts (e.g., *I can have only limited success*). We all have millions of thoughts. What gets us into trouble is when we *believe* them. For example, let's pretend I have the thought, *I am stupid!* At that moment, if I believe that thought, my whole state of being immediately shifts to a weakened negative self-perception and experience of myself. This could be manifested by other negative thoughts about myself, like: *What is my problem?* and *I can't believe I did that!* My emotions slide into negativity such as feelings of anger, fear, and sadness. These emotions can set off behaviors (for example, speaking from a place of anger or fear, confronting someone, slamming a door). Over time, our body and brain slowly become eroded from these toxic influences. A general rule of thumb: the calmer and more relaxed our survival brain areas are, the easier it will be for us to have some control over the direction of our thoughts. But even if our survival brain areas are still pretty extreme, we can still exert much control over which thoughts we buy into.

In these examples we saw that the thought was the beginning of the thread, which was followed by emotions and behaviors. Therefore, it is most effective to nip the thoughts in the bud! The moment you have bought into a negative or limiting thought and don't nip it in the bud or correct it, it is sort of like the horse getting out of the barn; it's way harder to deal with once it has translated to a negative emotion and behavior. Again, work with the thought ASAP! This becomes easier with more practice, and the quieter the ancient survival brain areas become. The reason it becomes easier and easier over time is that, at a much deeper level, we now "get it" that we are not our thoughts.

As we saw earlier, we are not our thoughts or emotions or beliefs! Our thoughts, emotions, and beliefs co-exist with our Essential Self; but our Essential Self transcends them all.

Here are a few of the many ways to support ourselves in this direction. The first four are practices that we can master on our own. The last is a technique for which we will need the help of a therapist.

Thought Stopping

We've already looked at this but let's examine it a bit more. Basically, thought stopping means to catch the negative thought or belief, challenge it, and actively let it go. There are many variations of how this can be practiced. The simplest is to catch a negative thought as soon as you notice it, then, when you recognize it is not true, just say "STOP!" and let it go! That means to just force it out of your conscious awareness and tell it "Goodbye!" But beware, because this can become much less effective if we do it by rote. When we do something by rote, it is no longer really connected to us, so it can lose much of its power.

Earlier, I described a variation of this, which is one of my favorites: the thought throw-out box. Yet another variation of this very simple technique is to place a rubber band loosely around your wrist. (Keep it loose enough that it doesn't at all interfere with blood or nerve supply. Ideally, it should be loose enough that it just hangs down your wrist.) Whenever you catch a negative thought about yourself, use your discernment to determine if the thought is true or not. If it is not true, lightly snap the rubber band on your wrist as you instruct the thought to leave. Again, people that have adequately calmed the limbic brain and brainstem should be able to fairly quickly let untrue negative thoughts fly away. When people find that they are just not sure if the negative thought is true or not, or they usually just can't let it go, they might need to calm the limbic/brainstem areas a bit more. Again, when our prefrontal cortex is being overrun by an overactive or underactive ancient survival brain area, the fight, flight, or freeze responses leads to a lot of our thinking becoming distorted and stuck. Then our power of discernment becomes impaired to one degree or another.

Internal Family Systems

See the full explanation of this technique on page 190.

The Sedona Method

This was one of the frameworks/models we looked at in Chapter 8. It bears revisiting now as it can also be used for clarifying and strengthening our prefrontal cortex function, whether or not we use it as a framework/model.

The Sedona Method is a great technique that you can learn from a book, CD, or by taking their training. Once you learn it, you can use it on your own for the rest of your life. It works primarily in the prefrontal cortex, so again, if someone's ancient survival brain areas are still too overactive, they can block much of the potential of this technique. You might first need to calm the limbic/brainstem areas to some degree before tackling this technique.

"The Work"

This technique from Byron Katie is explained in previous chapters. In addition to serving as a great framework, it is also a method of examining our thoughts and determining which ones are causing us to suffer in our lives. This also works primarily in the prefrontal cortex, so the same caveat applies about possibly needing some ancient survival brain calming first.

Twelve Steps

The twelve-step recovery method was also explained in the previous chapters.

This is another one of those practices to avoid doing in a rote manner. Once something becomes a habit, we lose much of our mindful attention to it. It is this conscious full reckoning with each of these questions and practices that opens our discernment, and helps to clear the way in the direction of the Essential Self.

As said earlier, there are many self-help techniques out there. We have covered just a few.

Cognitive Behavioral Therapy

This final approach to dealing with negative or limiting thoughts is the one that requires a therapist. It's called cognitive behavioral therapy (CBT) and it can be quite helpful if you want to work with a therapist, and/or you're not able to adequately help yourself with the aforementioned or other techniques. There are many types of CBT and skilled CBT therapists around the world.

The clearer you become that you are not your thoughts, the

easier it is for your Essential Self to surface. And, again, why should you care about your Essential Self surfacing? Because life feels a whole lot better when you identify with your Essential Self instead of your thoughts, emotions, and Deep False Beliefs. Thoughts, emotions, and beliefs very often take us on roller-coaster rides. I don't know about you, but I've had enough roller-coaster rides in my life!

The crux of it is this; the more you stop, question, and challenge the truth of your thoughts, the greater the space becomes between the thought and your buying into it.

The crux of it is this; the more you stop, question, and challenge the truth of your thoughts, the greater the space becomes between the thought and your buying into it.

As soon as you stop buying into a Deep False Belief or negative thought about yourself, it loses most of its toxic influence on you. The roller-coaster ride begins to glide to a stop.

Key Points

1. As we calm the ancient survival brain areas, some areas of the brain cortex become more available to us.

2. Some of these cortical areas are able to create better opportunities to reconnect with the Essential Self.

Principle of Essential Living

- *Our brain contains portals to access our Essential Self. Strengthening certain brain areas can facilitate reconnecting with our Essential Self.*

Chapter 11

Let the Sun Shine In

"It's not the years in your life that count.
It's the life in your years!"

—Abraham Lincoln

T he final two brain areas we will consider are the medial prefrontal cortex and the parietal cortex. We already talked about the medial prefrontal cortex earlier, but this is such an important brain area for supporting reconnecting with our Essential Self that we will take a closer look. Areas of the parietal cortex play a fascinating role with the veils being lifted off of our Essential Self.

Medial Prefrontal Cortex

The medial (middle) prefrontal cortex is located right in the middle of the prefrontal cortex. Take a look at the diagram on the next page to better understand its location.

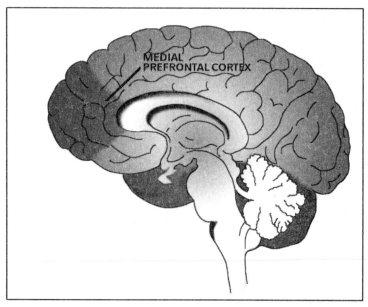

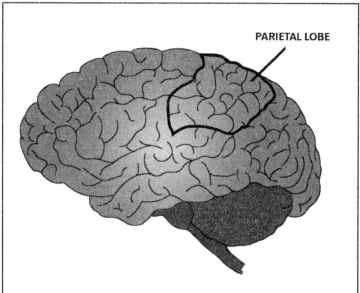

Figure 14: Other Relevant Areas of the Cortex:
The Medial Prefrontal Cortex and the Parietal Cortex.

What we now know is that the medial prefrontal cortex, and some nearby brain areas, have direct connections with areas of the limbic brain, including the amygdala, that sets off our fight, flight, and some of the freeze responses. Being so ancient in origin, and having a severely outdated "operating system," these limbic areas often fire when the stimulus is not a real threat, and/or fires way too strongly for the circumstances. If areas of the limbic brain are left to their own devices, they will frequently leave the person with startle responses, fears, terror, anger, and/ or certain freeze responses that are often way out of context to whatever the person is reacting to.

However, there is "wiring" from the medial prefrontal cortex that can give these limbic areas information that it is safe to calm down, etc. The medial prefrontal cortex can become more and more effective working with the limbic areas in this way. Over time, the medial prefrontal cortex can actually grow larger, and become increasingly better skilled at coaching and training these limbic areas.

What facilitates this growth? One of the potentially strongest influences that powerfully helps to expand the medial prefrontal cortex in this capacity are mindfulness practices. These can be in the form of mindfulness meditation, yoga, Tai Chi, and many other practices that involve being mindful of the felt sense.

As the limbic areas becomes less and less reactive, they cease to so frequently throw the switch that instructs the brainstem to start a fight, flight, or freeze reaction. Thereby, the brainstem can also calm down and become better regulated. *As the limbic*

areas calm, and the brainstem becomes better regulated, the pre-
frontal cortex, including the medial prefrontal cortex, become
more and more online. The functions on the list below that you
have seen a few times before now have the potential to open
and blossom more.

- Paying attention, observing, analyzing, organizing, logic, basic understanding, sense of time, planning, anticipating.

- Representational memory, the "story" of our lives, personality.

- Impulse control, inhibiting actions that are not appropriate, some emotional regulation, self-control.

- The context of an experience, some of our social skills, ability to mediate, negotiate, and weigh possible judgments.

- Empathy, ethics, morality, wisdom, personal will, intentions.

- Higher Consciousness: access to a sense of joy, peace, love, acceptance (not resignation), sense of oneness, serenity, equanimity, even-mindedness, sense of "all is well" (even if it is not), altruism (but not when it is from a "should"), ability to surrender to something greater than ourselves, gratitude, etc.

**Figure 15: Some Functions of the
Prefrontal Cortex in Humans.**

If you look at the bottom of the list, you'll see where it says "Higher Consciousness." These are other qualities of the Essential Self. Therefore, as we've seen before, our prefrontal cortex is one of the areas that *facilitates our accessing* our Essential Self. Let's look at one more area of our brain cortex that also facilitates our accessing our Essential Self—the parietal cortex.

The Parietal Cortex

This is the final area of the brain we will look at. In some ways we've saved the best for last. See Figure 14 (page 214) for its location. The parietal cortex has millions of circuits. The main function we'll focus on here is its creation of our sense of separateness from everything. When it is doing its job right, we perceive and experience ourselves to be totally separate from each other, and from everything else; we perceive that we are clearly delineated from everything around us from birth through death.

But as we increasingly get back in touch with our Essential Self, we find that our true nature is not one of separateness. We become aware that there is a very real connectedness among all of us. This ultimately leads us to much greater levels of compassion and love. Check this out with your own experience. When you have deeply loved someone, do you get an inkling of what I am speaking about? People who have helped their ancient survival brain areas calm down adequately often describe a wonderful sense of oneness and connectedness with others. This sense is also commonly found in long-term meditators.[39, 40, 41]

Why does this happen? In a nutshell, every second, areas of the parietal lobe receive many millions of pieces of incoming sensory information from our bodies and the surrounding space. Like a super-fast and super-powerful computer, it processes all of this incoming sensory information and creates the appearance and sense of very distinct boundaries between ourselves and what is around us. This ultimately leaves us with an overall sense of being disconnected from everything and everyone.

Now here's the really interesting part: in people who have consistently done meditation practices that have significantly calmed the ancient survival parts of their brain, and increased the function of other brain areas, the blood flow to these specific regions of the parietal lobes begins to *decrease*. As this occurs, the person becomes increasingly aware of their interconnectedness with others and everything around them. That connectedness with others that so many people want is actually an inherent part of our Essential Self. It is revealed when our nervous system feels safe and calm enough to allow the doors of our perception to open. [42, 43, 44, 45, 46]

The doors of perception to our Essential Self do not open through the intellect or our thinking. One of the ways they open is when our brain feels safe and allows us to deeply relax and become quiet inside.

The doors of perception to our Essential Self do not open through the intellect or our thinking. One of the ways they open is when our brain feels safe and allows us to deeply relax and become quiet inside.

Why are we wired this way? Once again, I think the answer always boils down to survival brain wiring. No matter what our higher brain functioning is potentially capable of understanding, experiencing, and opening to, the brakes of our ancient survival wiring usually need to be addressed first.

No matter what our higher brain functioning is potentially capable of understanding, experiencing, and opening to, the brakes of our ancient survival wiring usually need to be addressed first.

In summary, as the brainstem becomes increasingly regulated, and the limbic brain and brainstem cease to be stuck in fight, flight, and/or freeze, the prefrontal cortex, parietal cortex and some other brain areas begin to become the leader of our brain more often. When this happens, we may notice the following qualities, which are in addition to the five qualities of the Essential Self that we covered earlier in the book, i.e., a deep sense of peace, happiness, a strong sense of freedom, a strong sense of connectedness, and a capacity for profound love.

These are some of the same and other qualities that we have looked at, are inherent in our most basic nature. We all have them to at least some degree:

Resilient inner strength

Greater wisdom (I do not mean IQ; people can have wisdom and have an IQ that is low, medium, or high.)

Greater calm

An increased sense of well-being

An inner stillness

A sense of feeling freer

A greater sense of inner peace

More empowered

More spontaneous

A greater sense of connectedness with others and with
life itself

Increased happiness

More loving of self and others

Perceiving everything through a lens of truth

And much more . . .

To review, the first part of the Big Game Plan was stabilization for people who need or want it. Then we looked at potential frameworks/models, followed by Calling Off the Dogs, and empowering other brain areas.

The final item for our Big Game Plan is practicing good self-care. This enables us to carry out everything covered in this book. You can only be as effective as your body, mind, and spirit are capable of. We may have no control over certain types of illnesses, physical and mental limitations, etc.; however, we can maximize and optimize whatever cards we were dealt in our life. It is the practice of good self-care that enables us to be maximally effective in however we choose to live our lives. As described here, practice good self-care throughout! This will support us on our journey. This doesn't mean to become too focused on it. We want to eat right, not just for taking care of our body, but also because of how certain foods affect our brain. We want to stop any addictions, as they can short circuit our proceeding with our "big game plan." Things like sleeping adequately are also important, as sleep deprivation can easily lead us away from the path we are choosing. *Just don't mistake practicing good self-care as the path itself. Many folks do this! Just take good care of yourself.* For example, figure out the foods you are going to eat and not eat, put it into practice, and then forget about it.

To that end, one of the last areas about self-care that I want to cover a bit more because it is so widespread.

Avoid Intensity!

In our culture, we typically strive for "the best" in everything! When we go to a restaurant, we want the tastiest food, the best tasting beverages, etc. We want the best clothes, cars, homes, lifestyle that we can afford. There is nothing wrong with this! But, a good practice for assisting your lower survival brain areas in staying calm is to avoid intensity. As stated earlier, Ralph Waldo Emerson said, "Moderation in all things." For the limbic brain, which is the seat of intensity, cravings, addictions, urges, drives, etc., this is a wise recommendation. This would also apply to so much of the intensity addiction we are seeing around our country: extreme sports, extreme cycling, jumping off cliffs in wing suits, jumping off a building with a parachute, running ultramarathons in the desert, and so on. All of this is over stimulating to the limbic system, which revs us up, and we lose access to our Essential Self. Adrenaline, and other stress hormones and chemicals, alter our baseline of calm, which is what we need to access our Essential Self.

Here's something else I have found helpful for good self-care: cutting way, way down on listening to and watching the news. I read one news magazine each week to stay current on what's happening—that's it! Most of us are on a steady daily diet of very intense and disturbing news, and with the twenty-four-hour news cycle and social media, we're bombarded with it. You really don't need that much threatening and negative information each day, and your brain will likely function better with less of this type of stimulation. The same with too much attention to politics; we tend to get revved up with this, and it does our brain and body no good. Remember, our ancient survival brain areas have no sense of time and space. These functions are located in the prefrontal cortex, which had not yet evolved. Therefore, when the ancient survival brain areas are repeatedly exposed to horrific news, they cannot distinguish between violence and other problems somewhere else in the world, especially those not involving you. In this case, the chronically activated limbic response of fight, flight, freeze keeps us from our Essential Self.

There are many additional ways we expose ourselves to too much intensity. Keep your eyes open for them. If you have become addicted to intensity or are an adrenaline junkie, the treatment for this is the same as any other addiction: abstinence. Will you go through withdrawal? Probably yes. But the freedom you gain when you come out the other side may be worth it.

Now that we have a better organized brain, our thinking

brain is free to offer real clarity and the ability for sustained reflection. This is essential for identifying and clarifying what is most important to us and what is true for us. Also, as our survival brain areas calm and become more organized, areas in our parietal cortex may begin to lift veils that were covering our Essential Self.

One final note: we do not know exactly where our Essential Self resides in the brain, or if it doesn't reside in the brain. We do know that areas such as the prefrontal cortex and parietal cortex facilitate access. There has also been much speculation over many years concerning the role of the pineal gland and the Essential Self; or soul. The bottom line, however, is that we just don't know. Stay tuned!

Key Points

1. The medial prefrontal cortex (medial PFC), and related areas, are part of the brain cortex (outer shell of the brain) that can potentially help the ancient survival brain areas calm down significantly.

2. This medial PFC has strong potential for *plasticity*. This means that this part of the brain can grow larger and become increasingly influential on the ancient survival brain areas.

3. Mindfulness practices strengthen the medial PFC. These include yoga, Tai Chi, mindfulness meditation, and many more.

4. Another area of the outer shell of the brain is called the parietal cortex. This contains regions called the "orientation association areas." These potentially enable us to directly experience some of the inherent qualities of our Essential Self. But this brain area usually will not provide this function unless the ancient survival brain areas and certain other brain areas are very calm.

5. A common pitfall in our culture is that intensity is viewed in a positive light. But for brain and body function, too much intensity is not good; it tends to reactivate those ancient survival brain areas back into overactivity and can keep us stuck in "overdrive" or shut down. This can short circuit or limit our access to our Essential Self.

6. Practicing good self-care is an invaluable tool for keeping steady and centered on our path. However, be vigilant to not make good self-care the path itself! We want good self-care to serve us; not the other way around!

Essential Principle

- *The doors of perception to our Essential Self do not open through the intellect or our thinking. They open when our brain feels safe and becomes quiet enough.*

Chapter 12

A Summary of the Essential Principles

All of these principles are stated within various chapters of the book. As I experience them, these principles are underlying truths that I have come to see over the years. I think they are important enough to list together in one place. It is my sense that these are the very backbone of the book. The flow of these principles is also easier to follow as they are sequentially listed here.

Most people are not aware of what they most deeply want.

It is essential that we clarify what we want most. This can determine our life's direction.

Ultimately, we all want the same thing—to reconnect with our Essential Self (our true and inherent nature).

Some of the qualities that are inherent to the Essential Self are peace, joy, a sense of connectedness or unity, a sense of freedom, truth, and love.

Our Essential Self is who we are no matter what; we don't earn it, learn it, buy it, grow into it, or achieve it. We are born with it and we will die with it, unchanged.

At a very young age, the human brain powerfully turns our attention away from our Essential Self, and toward our outer world.

As a child, our mind, which is mainly a product of the survival brain programming, becomes fascinated with the outside world. It is far more intensely emotionally charged, both positively and negatively, than our Essential Self's quiet state of being. We become captivated by our outside world and our mind loves this!

We lose conscious connection with our Essential Self. We forget who we are. We begin to suffer. This is caused by an evolutionary glitch.

We unconsciously search for that which we already are— our Essential Self.

We don't notice our true self, our very essence, even though it is right in front of us, because our mind is too intense to notice the quiet and still Essential Self.

We unknowingly seek reconnection with our Essential Self through success in external things, such as relationships, work, prosperity, etc.

Attaining success in these areas cannot substitute for reconnecting with our Essential Self. We still suffer.

To the degree we consciously connect with our Essential Self, we have peace, happiness, a sense of freedom, a sense of unity, love, and truth. To the degree we are not connected with our Essential Self, we suffer.

As we reconnect with our Essential Self, there is a call to action to integrate our Essential Self into all areas of our lives.

Symptoms (suffering) can be a good thing! It motivates us to take action.

The Way Back: We *relax* into our Essential Self. We don't earn it, learn it, buy it, grow into it, or achieve it.

We are not our thoughts, emotions, or beliefs! Our thoughts, emotions, and beliefs have nothing to do with our Essential Self. Our Essential Self transcends all of these.

The more we stop identifying as our thoughts, the easier it is to calm the survival brain areas. The more we calm the survival brain areas, the easier it is to stop identifying as our thoughts.

Our brain contains ancient circuits that block access to our Essential Self. Reconnecting with our Essential Self may be facilitated by quieting and calming these ancient circuits.

Our brain contains portals to access our Essential Self. Strengthening certain brain areas can facilitate reconnecting with our Essential Self.

The doors of perception to our Essential Self do not open through the intellect or our thinking. They open when our brain feels safe and quiet enough.

"Barn's burned down.
Now I can see the moon."

—Mizuta Masahide,
Japanese Samurai warrior and poet, circa 1680

Endnotes

1. Maslow, Abraham H. *Motivation and Personality*. New York: Harpers, 1954. Print.

2. Maslow, Abraham H. *A Theory of Human Motivation*. Mansfield Center, CT: Martino Publishing, 2013. Print.

3. Bienenstock, E., & von der Malsburg, C. (1986). Statistical Coding and Short-Term Synaptic Plasticity: A Scheme for Knowledge Representation in the Brain. In E. Bienenstock, F. Fogelman, & G. Weisbuch (Eds.), *Disordered Systems and Biological Organization* (pp. 247–272). Les Houches, France: Springer-Verlag.

4. Felitti, Vincent J., M.D., Robert F. Anda, M.D., Dale Nordenberg, M.D., David F. Williamson, Ph.D, Alison M. Spitz, MPH, Valerie Edwards, BA, Mary P. Koss, Ph.D., and James S. Marks, M.D. "Relationship of Childhood Abuse and Household Dysfunction to Many of the Leading Causes of Death in Adults: The Adverse Childhood Experiences (ACE) Study." *American Journal of Preventative Medicine* 14.4 (1988): 245–58. Web.

5. Dhabhar, Firdaus. "Stress, Anxiety, and Susceptibility to Squamous Cell Carcinoma: Role of Immune Mediators." *The Official Journal of the International Society of Psychoneuroendocrinology* 71 (2016): 1–2. Web.

6. Gärling, Tommy, Amelie Gamble, Filip Fors, and Mikael Hjerm. "Emotional Well-Being Related to Time Pressure, Impediment to Goal Progress, and Stress-Related Symptoms." *Journal of Happiness Studies* 17.5 (2016): 1789–799. *Springer Link*. Web. 27 Feb. 2017.

7. Covey, Stephen. *The Seven Habits of Highly Effective People*. New York: Free Press, 1990. Print.

8. Mellody, Pia, Andrea Wells Miller, and Keith Miller. *Facing Codependence: What It Is, Where It Comes from, How It Sabotages Our Lives*. New York, NY: HarperOne, 2003. Print.

9. Mellody, Pia, Andrea Wells. Miller, and Keith Miller. *Facing Love Addiction: Giving Yourself the Power to Change the Way you Love*. New York: HarperOne, 2010. Print.

10. Mellody, Pia, and Lawrence S. Freundlich. *The Intimacy Factor: the Ground Rules for Overcoming the Obstacles to Truth, Respect, and Lasting Love*. San Francisco, CA: HarperSanFrancisco, 2004. Print.

11. Mellody, Pia, and Andrea Wells. Miller. *Breaking Free: A Recovery Workbook for Facing Codependence*. San Francisco: Harper & Row, 1989. Print.

12. Katie, Byron, and Stephen Mitchell. *Loving What Is: Four Questions That Can Change Your Life*. New York: n.p., 2003. Print.

13. Low, Abraham A. *Mental Health Through Will-Training: A System of Self-Help in Psychotherapy as Practiced by Recovery, Inc.* Boston: Christopher Pub. House, 1967. Print.

14. W., Bill. *Alcoholics Anonymous: The Story of How Many Thousands of Men and Women Have Recovered from Alcoholism*. 1st ed. New York City, NY: Works Publishing Company, 1939. Print.

15. Kabat-Zinn, Jon. *Mindfulness for Beginners*. Sounds True, 2006. CD.

16. Brach, Tara. *Radical Acceptance: Guided Meditations*. Tara Brach Productions, 2007. CD.

17. Hanh, Thich Nhat. *The Art of Mindful Living: How to Bring Love, Compassion, and Inner Peace into Your Daily Life*. Sounds True, 2000. CD.

18. Kornfield, Jack. *Guided Meditation: Six Essential Practices to Cultivate Love, Awareness, and Wisdom*. Sounds True, 2007. CD.

19. Young, Shinzen. *The Science of Enlightenment*. Sounds True, 1998. CD.

20. Craig, Gary. "This Is the Home for Official EFT™ (Emotional Freedom Techniques)." *The EFT Tapping Home*. n.p., n.d. Web. 27 Feb. 2017. http://www.emofree.com/.

21. Emerson, David, and Elizabeth Hopper. *Overcoming Trauma through Yoga: Reclaiming Your Body*. Berkeley, CA: North Atlantic, 2011. Print.

22. "HeartMath." *HeartMath*. n.p., n.d. Web. 27 Feb. 2017. http://www.heart-math.com/.

23. Weil, Andrew. *Breathing: The Master Key to Self Healing*. Sounds True, 1999. CD.

24. Maurer, Robert. *One Small Step Can Change Your Life: The Kaizen Way*. New York: Workman Publishing, 2014. Print.

25. Duhigg, Charles. *The Power of Habit: Why We Do What We Do in Life and Business*. New York: Random House Trade Paperbacks, 2014. Print.

26. Blumenthal, James A., Mats Fredrikson, Cynthia M. Kuhn, Ross L. Ulmer, Margaret Walsh-Riddle, and Mark Appelbaum. "Aerobic Exercise Reduces Levels of Cardiovascular and Sympathoadrenal Responses to Mental Stress in Subjects Without Prior Evidence of Myocardial Ischemia." *The American Journal of Cardiology* 65.1 (1990): 93–98. *Science Direct*. Web. 27 Feb. 2017.

27. Hinkley, James Matthew, Adam R. Konopka, Miranda K. Suer, and Matthew P. Harber. "Short-Term Intense Exercise Training Reduces Stress Markers and Alters the Transcriptional Response to Exercise in Skeletal Muscle." *American Journal of Physiology* (2016): n. pag. *APS Journals*. Web. 27 Feb. 2017.

28. Linehan, Marsha. "The Linehan Institute | Home." *The Linehan Institute | Home*. n.p., n.d. Web. 27 Feb. 2017. http://linehaninstitute.org/.

29. Linehan, Marsha M. *DBT Skills Training Manual*. New York: The Guilford Press, 2015. Print.

30. Stone, Meg. "Home." *Impact Boston*. n.p., n.d. Web. 27 Feb. 2017. http://impact boston.com/.

31. McClure, Deimante, BA, Samantha C. Greenman, BA, Siva Sundeep Koppolu, MBBS, Varvara Maria, MD, Zimri Yaseen, MD, and Igor I. Galynker, MD, PhD. "A Pilot Study of Safety and Efficacy of Cranial Electrotherapy Stimulation in Treatment of Bipolar II Depression." *The Journal of Nervous and Mental Disease* 203.11 (2015): 827–35. Web.

32. Mischoulon, David, Marasha F. De Jong, Ottavio V. Vitolo, Cristina Cusin, Christina M. Dording, Albert S. Yeung, Kelley Durham, Susannah R. Parkin, Maurizio Fava, and Darin D. Dougherty. "Efficacy and Safety of a Form of Cranial Electrical Stimulation (CES) as an Add-on Intervention for Treatment-Resistant Major Depressive Disorder: A Three Week Double Blind Pilot Study." *Journal of Psychiatric Research* 70 (2015): 98–105. Web.

33. Rose, Karen M., PhD, RN, Ann Gill Taylor, EdD, RN, FAAN, Cheryl Bourguignon, PhD, RN, Sharon W. Utz, PhD, RN, and Lisa E. Goehler, PhD. "Cranial Electrical Stimulation Potential Use in Reducing Sleep and Mood Disturbances in Persons with Dementia and Their Family Caregivers." *Fam Community Health* 31.3 (2008): 240–46. *HHS Public Access*. Web. 27 Feb. 2017.

34. Shapiro, Francine. *Eye Movement Desensitization and Reprocessing (EMDR): Basic Principles, Protocols, and Procedures*. 2nd ed. New York: Guilford Press, 2001. Print.

35. Levine, Peter. "Trauma Healing—Somatic Experiencing Trauma Institute." n.p., n.d. Web. 27 Feb. 2017. *www.TraumaHealing.org.*

36. Kluetsch, R. C., T. Ros, J. Théberge, P. A. Frewen, V. D. Calhoun, C. Schmahl, R. Jetly, and R. A. Lanius. "Plastic Modulation of PTSD Resting-State Networks and Subjective Wellbeing by EEG Neurofeedback." *Acta Psychiatrica Scandinavica* 130.2 (2014): 123–36. *Wiley Online Library*. Web. 27 Feb. 2017.

37. "EGGER." *EEG Education and Research*. n.p., n.d. Web. 27 Feb. 2017. *eeg spectrum.com.*

38. Rabin, Roni Caryn. "A Glut of Antidepressants." *The New York Times*. n.p., 12 Aug. 2013. Web.

39. Benson, Herbert, and Robert K. Wallace. "The Physiology of Meditation." *Scientific American* 226.2 (1972): 84–90. *APA PsycNet*. Web. 27 Feb. 2017.

40. Benson, Herbert, and Miriam Z. Klipper. *The Relaxation Response*. New York, NY: Quill, 2001. Print.

41. Davidson, Richard J. "Research." *Richard J. Davidson*. n.p., n.d. Web. 27 Feb. 2017. *http://richardjdavidson.com/.*

42. Newberg, Andrew B., and Mark Robert. Waldman. *How God Changes your Brain: Breakthrough Findings from a Leading Neuroscientist.* New York: Ballantine Trade Paperbacks, 2010. Print.

43. Newberg, Andrew B. *The Metaphysical Mind: Probing the Biology of Philosophical Thought.* San Bernardino, CA: CreateSpace Independent Publishing Platform, 2014. Print.

44. Newberg, Andrew B. *How Enlightenment Changes Your Brain: The New Science of Transformation.* New York: Avery Publishing Group, 2017. Print.

45. Newberg, Andrew B. *Principles of Neurotheology.* New York: Routledge, Taylor & Francis Group, 2016. Print.

46. Newberg, Andrew B., Eugene D'Aquili. *Why God Won't Go Away.* New York: Ballantine Books, 2001. Print.

About the Author

D R. SHELLEY URAM is a Harvard trained, triple board-certified psychiatrist and a Distinguished Fellow of the American Academy of Child & Adolescent Psychiatry. She was a Clinical Fellow at Harvard Medical School, and she completed her internship, residency, and chief residency at Massachusetts General Hospital, and a fellowship at Cambridge Hospital.

She speaks around the country about psychological trauma and how it often interferes with our ability to thrive in life. She is best known for communicating very complex information in an interesting and easy to understand manner.

Dr. Uram is a Clinical Associate Professor of Psychiatry at the University of Arizona College of Medicine and is a Senior Fellow at The Meadows in Wickenburg, Arizona.

Index